Do Over

Why it will work now when it didn't work then.

The Ignored, Underestimated, and Unknown Steps to Producing Results that I Didn't Learn by Reading Self-Help Books

By Matt Theriault

AuthorHouse™
1663 Liberty Drive
Bloomington, IN 47403
www.authorhouse.com
Phone: 1-800-839-8640

First published by AuthorHouse 11/2/2010

ISBN: 978-1-4520-8695-8 (sc)
ISBN: 978-1-4520-8694-1 (e)

Library of Congress Control Number: 2010914824

Printed in the United States of America

This book is printed on acid-free paper.

CONTENTS

PREFACE

Since the age of fifteen when I was working as a cart boy at Rancho San Joaquin Golf Course in Irvine, California, I knew that writing a book was in my future. I envisioned that it would manifest itself when I reached a point where I could look back on a life of reverence, prosperity, and contribution. My first book was to be one of marvelous retrospect, one of compelling recollection that the likes of Bill Gates, Donald Trump, and Warren Buffet would envy. My Great American Novel, the one that would share shelf space with *The Great Gatsby, Slaughterhouse-Five,* and *To Kill a Mockingbird* in distinguished libraries across the globe, was to be my first effort. I was convinced my first book would be a home run.

Over the years I have intermittently shared this vision with family, friends, and associates, and it was not until August 2008 that a seed was planted by the words of a complete stranger — a seed that would blossom almost overnight and not only transform my adolescent vision, but alter the course of my life.

For the purpose of this book, my story begins in 1987. This was the year I discovered motivational tapes. Out of nothing more than fascination and curiosity, I ordered Tony Robbins' *Personal Power* from a late-night infomercial. I remember watching the infomercial and wondering, "What in the hell is this?" I didn't know what a motivational or self-help program was, nor did I have any idea what Tony Robbins was selling. What I did know, after several viewings of the infomercial, was that I wanted it — I had to have it — but I still had no idea what I was about to buy. I bought it anyway.

A few days later the Tony Robbins package arrived. I ripped it open and proceeded to cram the 30-day program into a week. Each day I listened to the program I felt better than I had the previous day. I felt unstoppable. The *Personal Power* program caused me to look at life in an entirely different way. Rather than looking at my life in terms of a traditional existence (go to school, get good grades, graduate from a credible college, and get a solid job), I began to see a life where anything I set my sights on was possible.

After completing *Personal Power*, my awareness of the personal development industry began to broaden. I began to listen to, and read other programs by, Earl Nightingale, Tom Hopkins, Brian Tracy, Norman Vincent Peale, and the "godfather" of personal development, Napoleon Hill. It was Hill's thirteen principles from *Think and Grow Rich* (specifically the quote, "What the mind can conceive and believe, it can achieve"), Earl Nightingale's *Lead the Field,* and Tony Robbins' *Personal Power* that resonated the most with me. Earl, Napoleon, and Tony were the catalysts for major changes in my life. I soon learned that, if not for my exposure to these teachers, my future would almost certainly have been one of mediocrity.

From that point — at age 18 — my mantra was, "If I can see it, I can be it." The life of a dreamer, an independent thinker, a self-starter, a motivator, and an entrepreneur had begun.

My passion was music. Specifically, hip-hop music. I started a record label and music distribution company. Initially, I composed and produced instrumental tracks in a makeshift bedroom studio and solicited my friends and local artists to rap and sing on my instrumentals. I had compiled an extensive library of singles, EPs, and LPs. I designed the artwork for these projects, pressed them up on 12" vinyl, and once a week drove a Southern California route of independent music stores selling my music out of the trunk of my car. Soon I found myself distributing other labels' releases on my weekly route. Over the next few years, my little company attracted the attention of Bill Baren at TRC Distribution (a mid-sized music distributor specializing in dance and hip-hop music) in San Francisco. Later, I connected with Michael Bull of Caroline Distribution (EMI) in New York. For fifteen years, my momentum was moving in the right direction until my passion-turned-profitable-business came to a screeching halt due to rapidly emerging business models and technology. If "video killed the radio star," the digital download killed the compact disc distributor.

My life as a music mogul had been reduced to an average rise-and-fall story. To be more precise, from beginning to end my time in the music business was more like an amusement park rollercoaster ride than it was a smooth jet flight that ascends, cruises, and descends. My journey in the music industry was one of radical peaks and dramatic valleys. I was fortunate to experience stellar results, yet *consistent* success eluded me. Something was amiss. Even when times were good, something was missing. I had grown so accustomed to the persistent and imminent free-fall lurking just around the bend that I never completely enjoyed the good times, nor did they ever really last long enough to enjoy.

My first attempt at being an entrepreneur came to a disappointing end. Even as I write this book, those hard-knock lessons continue to sink in. My record label would likely be thriving today had I not:

1. Ignored the importance of planning the work and working the plan;
2. Ignored the virtues of integrity, poise, and loyalty;
3. Underestimated the value of a mentor and incorporating the wisdom of those who had been there;
4. Ignored the impact of my own thoughts, beliefs, and attitudes;
5. Underestimated the importance of continued education, constant practice, and scheduled evaluation.

In hindsight, I had no idea what I was doing. I didn't have a chance.

On the bright side, the school of hard knocks delivered an invaluable education that has served me in every area of my life since.

Although there are an abundance of personal development programs replete with lessons which, had I applied them, could have saved my record label and me from myself, there are concepts and techniques I have learned, embraced, and nurtured since then that I have yet to read in a book. It is these concepts and techniques that are making a significant difference my second time around as an entrepreneur, but the difference being made is not limited to business. These concepts and techniques are making a difference in every area of my life where my intention is to produce a specific, desired result. I am confident that these concepts and techniques will make a difference for you as well – regardless of what you are up to in life.

It was the simple words "You should write a book," spoken by a complete stranger, that inspired me to write this book. They were spoken by a person who had just attended a free workshop I had conducted for real estate agents, business associates, and friends.

By the end of that workshop, several of the guests mentioned to me they would have paid money for it, and that I absolutely needed to write a book about the processes involved in producing desired results. It was in that moment that I discovered the power of taking action on suggestions given to me. Since, I have discovered that taking action on those suggestions often produces results far greater than what was originally desired.

This book is a perfect illustration of those results.

First, I took the suggestion (from myself) to practice and to create for the sake of creating. I really just wanted to see if I could produce an arbitrary result using everything I had come to know (what is now evolved into the Do Over Plan). I achieved my *desired* result – the workshop. Then, I took the suggestions from guests at my workshop to write this book, which represents a result far greater than what I'd originally desired. Coincidentally, this result is often the outcome of the Do Over Plan.

I'd like to pass along three invaluable lessons that have come to me during the course of writing this book:

1. Writing this book has been a therapeutic and transforming experience. I ultimately decided to write it for two reasons: to share with humanity what I have learned from Hard Knock U; and to instill within me my life's invaluable lessons by teaching them. A wise man shared with me that the most effective way to learn something is to teach it as soon as you learn it. I pass that on to you. I encourage you to embrace the lessons of *Do Over* and teach them to someone else. By doing, so you will increase your retention of the system. The lessons will become a part of you, increasing the probability of your own success.

2. I encourage everyone to take on the endeavor of writing a book. I spent 15 years in the music industry and witnessed enough to leave me with the belief that everybody has at least one hit song (or at least one "hit" idea for a song) inside of them. I presume it is similar with regard to a great invention (or at least an idea for a great invention). I have come to believe that the same is true when it comes to a bestselling book (or an idea for a bestselling book). *Do Over* is my idea. Do you have one? I bet you do. Write a book.

3. And finally, there is nothing worse than the feeling of regret. Regret is a unique type of pain. It is a pain that nothing to which I have become privy can cure. In simple terms, regret is lost time that you wish you had spent differently. Time passed is time lost. It can never be retrieved. Each and every one of us will endure the pain of discipline or the pain of regret. Short-term pain creates long-term satisfaction, and short-term satisfaction more times than not leads to long-term pain. In my opinion, there is no comparison. There is a saying that an ounce of prevention is worth a pound of cure. I have come to learn the hard way that discipline prevents regret, of which there is no cure.

I conclude my preface to *Do Over* with the concept of regret because this book is your access to everything you have ever wanted, but as I have touched on, nobody is going to do it for you. You must try, or you will definitely experience regret. And you must try and try and try again until you succeed. The worst thing a human can do is not try. Whether it is a new invention you have been tinkering with, a new business you have been contemplating, an idea for a screenplay that has been hibernating in the back of your mind, or it is the next Great American Novel resting at your fingertips, to be aware of what you want and not pursue it, to spend years in silent hurt wondering what "could have been," is the absolute worst decision a human can make — for the result is regret.

Matt

INTRODUCTION

Given that I'm in the throes of my second go-round as an entrepreneur, the obvious title for this book was *Do Over*. I included the subtitle *Why It Will Work Now When It Didn't Work Then* because to make your Do Over effective you will first need to identify certain distinctions about the way you have been functioning that led to the need for a Do Over in the first place. After all, how you do *one* thing is how you do *everything*. The intent of this book is to offer distinctive steps you can take as you create your Do Over.

I have taken these steps. They work.

Some of the steps I'll discuss will be familiar to you, but you may have ignored them. Some of the steps you may have implemented but underestimated their value. Some of the steps you might not have known even existed. These steps helped me choose this book's second, descriptive subtitle: *The Ignored, Underestimated, and Unknown Steps to Producing Results*.

Webster's defines the word *ignored* accordingly: *to disregard on purpose*. Most people know exactly what to do in certain circumstances, but they often don't do what they know. Ignoring what you know to do will almost always result in the desired outcome being just out of reach.

Sometimers

In addition to those people who ignore what they know to do, there is another group of people who begin to take action with what they know to do, but they only partially commit to that action. I call them "Sometimers." Sometimers do just enough to get by and complain when they don't get the exact results they want. Some people become such masters at being Sometimers that they create the illusion that they're doing everything possible to achieve their intended goal. When success eludes them, these masters convince everyone around them (including themselves) that it is life's circumstances – not their lack of action – that is responsible for their goals never being fully reached. These people often use the phrases "bad luck" and "can't catch a break" to justify why they keep missing the mark. What most don't realize is that being a Sometimer and giving half their effort to any given goal is a formula for failure. Half-effort typically doesn't produce half-result. It almost always produces an outcome that is *less* than half of what was desired. What usually follows the Sometimer's poor results is an overwhelming feeling of helplessness. The reality is, "it" would likely have worked just fine. What prevented the goal being reached was that the Sometimer didn't work "it!"

Before I expound on the unknown steps, it's important to note that I do not purport I'm presenting steps that have never before been introduced. Quite the opposite is true. I'm not reinventing the wheel. I'm simply presenting proven success paradigms in my own way, as I appreciate the fact that it's possible my particular method of communication may resonate with people.

I reference the unknown in a figurative sense. For me, the unknown represents the fact that, after immersing myself in the world of personal development, the steps I knew I needed to take to ensure my success didn't really hit home with me until after nearly twenty years of study. Then, suddenly, everything I had ever read regarding the steps necessary to win in business – and in life – struck me as epiphanies. Once I began to experience actual positive results from having implemented these steps, the "Ah-ha!" moments seemed endless. But the "Ah-ha!" moments were there for the taking all along. I just hadn't made the choice to powerfully embrace the steps and let the epiphanies take their natural course.

I also recognize that there are certain truths about the human condition. One of them is that we all receive information differently, and that external factors play a large role in determining how we process the information we receive. In my case, it took nearly twenty years for me to really receive the information I'd been absorbing as it was intended to be received. I attribute the amount of time it took me to "get it" to my lack of maturity and my unwillingness to look at the things that made me uncomfortable.

Let me quickly tell you what this book is *not* about. This is not a book that will describe in painful detail how I was born in squalor and pulled myself out to now enjoy a millionaire lifestyle. This is also not a book about how many cars, boats, toys and houses I own, or about all of the wonderful, exotic vacations my family and I take.

What this book is about is much more important than any of those things. Besides, what I have accomplished, what I own, and the kind of lifestyle I live will not make the slightest difference in your life. What will make a difference is my commitment to sharing valuable information that can give you access to everything YOU have ever wanted. This book represents that commitment.

The concepts, techniques and systems I share in this book work. It's as simple as that. They can work for you when you choose to apply them. They work with unwavering consistency.

Knowledge Is Potential Power

The expression "knowledge is power" is embedded in our culture; however, that expression by itself is not entirely true — it is not complete. A more accurate revision could be "knowledge is <u>potential</u> power." Until knowledge is *applied*, it does not represent actual power. The same is true as it relates to the concepts detailed in this book. By themselves, these concepts will assuredly make a fun and intriguing read. However, if you do not take the commensurate action necessary to have these concepts make a difference, it is likely this book will have the same lack of effect as so many other feel-good, self-help books.

> It is in your moments of decision that your destiny is shaped.
>
> *—Tony Robbins*

Over the years, I've observed an unsettling common denominator in many (not all) humans: many people love to learn *how* to do something, but very few people approach the actual *doing* of something with similar enthusiasm. Which of these best describes you? Are you a perpetual student who loves to learn but are always convincing yourself that taking the time to learn just a little more will make everything magically click? Or are you the diligent student who recognizes that learning is an ever-evolving process, and you learn what is necessary to accomplish a specific goal and take action on what you've learned? Can you see a pattern in your life with respect to learning and doing? I certainly can. Here's the good news: if you have experienced the pattern of "loving-to-learn-and-not-doing," it does not mean that you are stuck with it. You have a choice.

Tony Robbins said it best: "It is in your moments of decision [choice] that your destiny is shaped." I want to draw your attention to two elements of this quote. First, it is in your "moments" of decision. A decision is not somewhere to get to. It does not take time to decide. A decision happens instantly, in a moment. For most people, that moment happens precisely when the discomfort of not deciding exceeds the discomfort of deciding. Second, it is *your* decision. Tony did not say that it is in *their* moments of decision your destiny is shaped; it is *your* decision. It is up to YOU. So, if the decision "to do" (or any decision for that matter) happens in a moment and it is your decision, isn't <u>now</u> the best time for you to decide?

Everything you want out of life is accessible out of your application of the techniques and disciplines in *Do Over*. So, decide. Decide that this is the last book you will read in search of your life's answers. Decide to do more than read. Decide to READ, LEARN and DO. The title of the book is *Do Over*, not *Learn Over*. I can show you the way (as can several authors, mentors, teachers, gurus and coaches), but only YOU can do it. None of the authors, mentors, teachers, gurus and coaches will do it for you.

It would not surprise me that, as you read this, you will begin to recognize that you have heard some of these ideas before. It is possible you have been exposed to some of these concepts several times in your life. Not only may you find yourself familiar with some of the ideas in this book, you will find this book brimming with time-honored wisdom. Why? Why would I include in my book that which has been written before? I have several answers for you:

1. It is possible that I am being presumptuous and this is your first exposure to personal development.
2. Perhaps you forgot.
3. Maybe you remember, but this is the time you actually "get it."
4. Maybe you "get it," but this is the time you actually "do it."
5. I see no need to reinvent what works (à la the wheel).
6. What works bears repeating and repeating. Repetition is the mother of learning. If you're not doing, you haven't learned and you deserve to hear it again.
7. The ignored, underestimated, and unknown steps to producing results are incomplete without a foundation – the basics. By bringing it all together, a powerful, effective and efficient system has been created for you, the Do Over Plan.

My Personal Do Over

You would not be reading this book if it were not for the Do Over Plan. This book is a product of the plan. Given the natural cynicism that has found its way into our society, I know that type of evidence would not be enough proof for most people. Most people want to see statistics. Most people want to see much bigger proof than a book. Most people want to be shown the money! My Do Over is young. I'm just getting started again. My current endeavors are new endeavors, yet are moving forward with extraordinary velocity. By the time *Do Over* is published, I will have caused everything listed below (and then some). So that you can check up on me and confirm the ideas, concepts and techniques embodied in this book, this is what I am up to in life:

1. Given the current opportunity the real estate market offers, I am building a multi-million-dollar real estate investment company, Albino Dino (www.AlbinoDino.com).
2. Per the wisdom of Donald Trump and Robert Kiyosaki, I am building a multi-million-dollar direct sales business, Epic Professionals (www.EpicProfessionals.com).
3. Following my passion for Americans helping Americans, I am gifting housing to New Orleans families displaced by Hurricane Katrina and creating financial literacy within the most impoverished communities of Louisiana (www.RebuildTheBayou.com).
4. Having discovered the positive impact of a mentor to one's success, I have launched an Internet resource business representing a plethora of mentors for the four areas of life: relational, spiritual, financial, and physical (www.VirtualMentorship.com).

How all of these things will be accomplished is unknown to me at this time, but that is part of the process (as you will read). It is not necessary to know "how" in the beginning. As long as you know "what," the Do Over Plan will take care of the "how." Getting started is the key!

The Do Over Plan does not necessarily express the way I wish the world to be, but the way it genuinely is. In other words, my system is based on reality as it applies to the human condition. Over the years I have found that most people, including myself at times, choose to ignore the unforgiving realities of life regardless of how pronounced the evidence to support such realities can be. For the Do Over Plan to work, you will need to work *it* with integrity. Success has been defined as the progressive realization of a worthy goal, an operative word being "worthy." Honest, ethical, truthful, moral, and honorable are synonymous with worthy. Pursuing a worthy goal without integrity leads to inevitable failure, and failure leads to grief. Integrity makes life work as it makes the Do Over Plan work.

Who is this book really for? You know how some people want to be successful, whether it's their first, second, third, or umpteenth time around the block, but no matter what they try it just never works out as they had hoped; or they simply don't know where to begin; or they don't have the time to pursue success because they're too busy trying to survive; or they don't have the money to launch their great idea; or they're plain and simply exhausted and have lost their bounce and inspiration to take the first step? When any of these circumstances come into play for an individual, it typically creates confusion or fear. A confused mind does nothing, and fear will literally stop people dead in their tracks. Life will continue to pass them by until one day they wake up dazed and confused, wondering what happened and where their life went.

I understand every single one of these scenarios because I have experienced them firsthand; yet I overcame every one of them. This book is my contribution to those who find themselves stopped. What you can expect to get from this book is:

- A new and empowering relationship with success and achievement;
- The elimination of your own destructive patterns;
- An understanding (and the elimination) of the seven toxins that kill success;
- An understanding (and the elimination) of your personal suppressive barriers;
- How to incorporate into your life the nine character traits of successful people;
- How to create a plan that inspires you and calls you powerfully into action;
- How to collapse timeframes and create quantum leaps during your pursuit of success;
- How to achieve your dreams and goals with greater ease than you had ever imagined by implementing the ignored, underestimated, and unknown steps to producing results.

Do Over doesn't draw on any formal studies or documentation. Its conclusions are derived from personal experience and observed corroboration. It is my goal to introduce to you the belief that if you had received this book's knowledge before your previous failed attempts, you might not have felt compelled to read a book titled Do

Over. It is my commitment that, from the moment you make the decision to take action and pursue what your mind has conceived for your Do Over, I will coach you through the process to your satisfaction. Your application of the Do Over Plan will turn your dreams into reality and do it faster than you had ever imagined.

Let's begin!

CHAPTER 1:
YOUR RELATIONSHIP TO SUCCESS

Before setting up a new plan for your Do Over, it is worth investigating what derailed you the last time around – to make sure that what went awry last time is not repeated this time. There is a saying, "How you do one thing is how you do everything." Consider how you drive to work, or how you eat your breakfast, or how you play basketball as clues to what will prevent success in your next endeavor. Kind of far-out, huh? Through these next few chapters, I will help you determine and eliminate what stopped or hindered your previous success. I refer to these obstacles as your "invisible barriers," some of which will be intrinsic, and some extrinsic. I will lead you through a few different inquiries by offering suggestions to help distinguish what has prevented (and likely consistently prevents) you from reaching the levels of success you desire. Once these invisible barriers are revealed, your consciousness will help you control them.

For this inquiry to be effective, I will need your participation.

The Cause of Failure

First, I will need you to consider that what you believe interfered with your success is *not* what interfered with your success. For example, if your last endeavor failed because a funding source fell through at the last minute, consider that it was not the funding source at all. Or if your last relationship failed because the mother-in-law would not stay out of your business, consider it was not the mother-in-law at all. The cause of failure may have been that funding source or mother-in-law, but I need you to be open to look elsewhere if we are going to reveal your invisible barriers. My request is to be open.

Trying on Sunglasses

Second, consider what I suggest during this inquiry. Just consider it. Play along. Think of this as trying on a pair of sunglasses. We are going to try on several pairs, look in the mirror, and decide if they fit. If they do not fit, you will put them back on the rack and try on a new pair. Are you with me? In other words, I will be offering suggestions and asking questions throughout this inquiry. When I ask a question – that is, when it's time to stop, try on the sunglasses, and consider them – be open and think. Answer the question to yourself. If something hits home, make a note of it. When the inquiry is complete, we will refer to these notes. If nothing comes up for you (if you do not like the way the sunglasses fit), then continue reading.

How Do You Define Success?

What is success? Literally, success is a favorable or prosperous conclusion to an endeavor. You'll notice there's nothing in that definition that says success is fame and fortune. It's simply the desirable completion of an attempt. Whatever the desired outcome of that attempt, it is entirely up to you, always. You get to choose your own definition of success. The root of most people's definition of success, however, is given to them by comparing themselves to others.

Regardless of how you came up with your current definition of success, what is your relationship to it? As previously mentioned in this book's introduction, success has been defined as the progressive realization of a worthy goal or ideal. Another operative word from this definition is "progressive." Success is progressive and ongoing. It is a journey. It is not a destination. There is nowhere to "get." It is an ongoing series of completed events. This is really important to understand because so many people delay their happiness for that day when they are successful. That day is not coming. Let me clarify, a day may come, but it will not last. That day is merely a break in the journey.

Here is what I mean. I have spoken to countless "successful" people and they all have this in common: they eventually ponder the question, "Is this all there is?" Typically, once they realize that "Yes, this is it," they resume the journey. So, a cardinal tenet of success is recognizing that it is a journey, and there is nothing for you to do other than *enjoy the ride!*

Given that everybody has different goals and ideals, the definition of success will be different for everybody. What you'll always want to stay in tune with is this: did you create your own definition of success, or did someone give it to you? Success is whatever you want it to be. Perhaps success relates to your profession, your hobby, your relationships, or your studies. You get to choose for you.

Many people unknowingly sabotage their success by comparing themselves to others. For example, let's say earning $100,000 a year is a successful level of earning for you – until you learn your neighbor earns $200,000. You then change your definition of success and strive to earn $200,000, until you learn your brother-in-law earns $300,000. You then set your eyes on $300,000 a year while you have yet to do what it takes to achieve $100,000. You now find yourself discouraged and so focused on someone else's definition of success that yours never manifests, or does, but never feels like it does. Many end up chasing the proverbial carrot. Comparing yourself to others is a journey that is impossible to enjoy. It leads to disappointment. Nothing is ever enough. Happiness and satisfaction will elude you if you compare your success to that of others. Define what success is to you, which I'll help you do a little later, and stick to it. Once you reach it, you can create a new definition. Whatever your definition of success may be, the principles set forth to achieve it apply impartially.

I think it is safe to say that everybody wants to be successful at something. The question is, how successful do we want to be? Moderately successful? Very successful? The most successful? Talent helps, but enthusiasm and persistence are key. In fact, just before I began to write *Do Over,* I finished reading *Talent is*

Overrated by Geoff Colvin, and I was left with the notion that although talent exists, it is irrelevant to higher achievement. This can be a pivotal revelation for most people, because most people have convinced themselves that they don't have what it takes to succeed. The suppressive influences (which I will address in detail later) that most people experience growing up could have conditioned you to believe that success is for the talented, the lucky, the privileged or the "already successful." If this is your belief, even remotely, read the chapter in Malcolm Gladwell's book _The Outliers_ about the 10,000 Hour Rule. You will never entertain that notion again.

Barriers to Success

With the pursuit of success so ingrained in our society, why do so few people achieve it? I have personally found that very few are prepared to make the sacrifices success takes. So many are in search of a solution, a method, a program, a coach, or a "silver bullet" way to become successful. There is no easy or instant solution. The only road to success is through consistent, focused action, mistakes—lots of mistakes—and refocused action. There are no shortcuts. It will be more work than you want to do, and depending on your goals, require more money than you want to spend. Enthusiasm and persistence, not talent or a magic "success" pill, will elevate you to the level of success to which you aspire. For the masses, being _liked_ is higher on their list of priorities, whether consciously or subconsciously, than being _successful_. A predominant need to be liked will hinder one's attainment of success. Strength and resilience are required. Most, when faced with a decision to stand their ground congruent with their goal, will not because they feel by doing so they will not be liked, which is a ridiculous belief. As Geoff Colvin writes in _Talent is Overrated_ (and I will concur), "being liked" is even more ridiculous. Success escapes the majority of people because they believe it takes talent to succeed; are endlessly searching for an easier way; and/or are being nice so that other people will like them. Do any or all of these apply to you? Regardless of the level of success you are striving for, your success will perpetually exceed your grasp as long as one of these three barriers is present.

Fear of Success

Here is a question worth asking: Are you afraid of success? Without hesitation most people would respond, "Are you crazy? If I were afraid of it, why would I be reading a book on how to attain it?" Maybe not, but that was my response the first time the question was asked of me. Then I looked a little deeper. After an honest self-inquiry, the question did not seem so absurd. Think about it. Earlier I drew your attention to how many do not achieve success because they are more concerned with being liked. Another reason so few achieve success is because they are unwilling to make the sacrifices required for its attainment. So, if you are afraid of not being liked, then you are essentially afraid of success. If you are unwilling to, or afraid of, making the necessary sacrifices, then you are afraid of success. Fear of success is an expression of inadequacy accompanied by the belief that we don't deserve to achieve. Further, guilt is often experienced when we do better than expected. When you feel inadequate or unworthy of success, you will repeatedly fall short, resulting in the curse of permanent potential.

So, are you afraid of success? If you have reluctantly changed your answer to "yes," don't worry. Later, I will show you how to use fear as a resource. You may even come to know fear as your most powerful ally. Imagine that!

Here is another inquiry: Do you deserve to succeed? You may be pursuing that worthy goal, but do you believe you are worthy enough to receive it? People tend to go through life with a sense of entitlement. I call this sense of entitlement your "deserve meter." Who you are today and how successful you are is in direct proportion to what you think you deserve. Is your deserve meter set above or below your goals? What you think you deserve will manifest itself. What do you think you deserve?

Whether you feel you do not have what it takes to succeed, you fear success, or you feel undeserving of success, the bottom line is you have a responsibility to succeed. People do not realize they can make a difference, and they are unaware it is their responsibility to do so. It is impossible to live a complete life unless you succeed. Your highest level of happiness will be found in the giving to loved ones. In order to give, you must have. In order to have, you must succeed. In his 1994 inaugural speech, Nelson Mandela addressed it all: fear, merit, contribution and responsibility:

"Our deepest fear is not that we are inadequate. Our deepest fear is that we are powerful beyond measure. It is our light, not our darkness that most frightens us. We ask ourselves, who am I to be brilliant, gorgeous, talented, fabulous? Actually, who are you *not* to be? You are a child of God. Your playing small does not serve the world. There is nothing enlightened about shrinking so that other people won't feel insecure around you. We are all meant to shine, as children do. We were born to make manifest the glory of God that is within us. It's not just in some of us; it's in everyone. And as we let our own light shine, we unconsciously give other people permission to do the same. As we are liberated from our own fear, our presence automatically liberates others."

— Marianne Williamson

It is your right and responsibility to succeed. Your family and loved ones deserve your success. You deserve it.

CHAPTER 2:
THE SEVEN TOXINS
THAT KILL SUCCESS

Now that we have established a mindset and your relationship to success, we will look deeper for that which will really make the difference. What we are looking for are your invisible barriers, both internal and external, that routinely hinder your progress. The objective is to bring these barriers into the light, into consciousness. By revealing your invisible barriers to yourself and continually increasing your awareness of their existence and how they impact your life and performance, they will wane and become little more than nuisances over which you will have control.

As before, we will conduct this inquiry with a series of suggestions injecting intermittent questions. Remember, we are going to try on these suggestions just like a new pair of sunglasses. If we do not like the way they fit, we will put them back on the rack and try on a new pair. Some will fit, and some will not. The objective is to find the sunglasses that fit while taking notes on each pair you try. When we have completed this initial inquiry, you should have a page or so of notes revealing your invisible barriers. Simply being aware of them will contribute to your future success. However, if you would like to explore further coaching on removing your invisible barriers, visit http://theDoOverGuy.com/coaching/.

I have suggested your relationship to success as an inquiry to help reveal some of your invisible barriers. Most people can start to see possible missteps they made in previous endeavors through their relationship to success. If nothing showed up for you in that inquiry, that's okay. We are only scratching the surface.

Let's continue the inquiry into what previously impeded your success. It is important because your Do Over Plan will be more effective if we first clear out the junk. In other words, if you were going to turn your attic into a guest bedroom, wouldn't it make sense to remove the old boxes, dust and sweep prior to moving in the new bedroom furniture? Out with the old and in with the new, as they say. This inquiry is just like that.

The Seven Toxins

Over the years I have been able to identify seven toxins that will almost assuredly destroy your success. When they are present, success is virtually impossible. What makes these toxins so dangerous is that they act and work like radon gas (my own personal metaphor). If you don't know, radon gas is silent, odorless, invisible, and it kills. These seven toxins can take your success in precisely the same way radon can take a life. Here is my countdown of the seven:

Toxin #1: Violating the Law of Being – Underrated

The natural order of success and achievement, or life in general for that matter, is:

BE – DO – HAVE

The law states that by focusing solely on "being" the person you desire to be, you will be compelled to "do" what that person would do, resulting in what that person would "have." If this book is anything but your first exposure to personal development, you almost certainly have heard of this law before (or a variation thereof).

The law of BE-DO-HAVE (I will sometimes refer to it as the "Law of Being") can almost be

> It is who we choose to be in the face of the journey that gives us power and performance, or not, in what we are committed to.
>
> – Andrew J. Norris, Ph.D.

categorized as common knowledge. If so, why mention it? Why take up the time, paper and ink to even reference it?

Because!

Because it is the first example of an underrated step, or more tragically, an ignored step. It is also a perfect example of "knowledge is <u>potential</u> power."

Just knowing is not enough. One must apply the knowledge to experience the power. The Law of Being is so powerful that if you were to stop reading right now and apply only it, you would not need to read any further.

But why should you read further? Because implementing this law is easier said than done. There are invisible barriers yet to be revealed to you that will undermine your ability to implement this law over time. The vast majority of our world's population, even the people who are familiar with this law, unknowingly violate it countless times per day. Disregarding this one law is literally the equivalent to swimming upstream, running against the wind or riding a bike up a hill. If life is treating you unfairly or is doling out tough lesson after tough lesson, if it feels like the world is against you, stop and look at who you are being.

Andrew J. Norris, Ph.D., an amazing mind, a coach and great friend, once said to me, "There's where we are and there's where we want to be. It is who we choose to be in the face of the journey that gives us power and performance, or not, in what we are committed to." Dr. Norris understands the Law of Being. To hear it from him, that is all there is — being — and I agree.

The Law of Being is akin to the Law of Gravity. It exists whether you believe in it or not. The Law of Gravity will not discriminate. If you were to jump off a building, gravity could not care less if you were good, bad, fat, skinny, old, young, rich, poor, dumb, or smart; gravity says you will hit the ground. The same is true with the Law of Being. It affects everyone the same.

The inquiry for you is, in what sequence are you applying the law? If you do not have everything you want, you're likely either living in one of two orders:

HAVE – DO – BE

DO – HAVE – BE

For example, if you *have* the nice car, you will *do* what it takes to keep it, and then you will *be* successful and happy. Or, you will *do* what you think it takes to *have* the nice car, and then you will *be* successful and happy.

You should understand by now that these are the "swimming upstream" versions of success and achievement. If you looked long and hard enough, you *may* find an exception to the rule, but would you not rather swim with the current to your success? The Law of Being says you are to *be* successful and happy first, which will compel you to *do* what successful and happy people do, resulting in *having* what successful and happy people have. Once applied in the order of BE-DO-HAVE, life will seem to unfold almost effortlessly. The question to ask and make note of is, "Who are you being most of the time?"

Toxin #2: Stress

Growing up, I remember my dad always saying, "You don't have to do anything but die and pay taxes." That is definitely one way to look at the world, and kept in its proper context I suppose it's accurate. Every time he said it, however, it caused me to think of additions to the list of "have-to-dos." It's been a lifelong personal game to see how many things I could add to the list.

As a kid, I came up with obvious things like eat and breathe. As an adult, I have come to understand the point of the statement as there is not a whole lot that we have to do in life. Most of what we experience as reality is imposed on us, such as paying taxes. Regardless of the number of items you can compile on your have-to-do list, one thing is for certain: there are very few certainties in life that apply to us all. One of the absolutes, however, is that each and every one of us will experience *stress*. It is not if, but when, and how often, and to what intensity?

Stress, under certain conditions, may produce a positive experience. It is not uncommon for one to respond to stress by calling on internal resources to produce results and accomplish goals. Referring to stress under these circumstances in a chapter titled "The Seven Toxins that Kill Stress" would not make much sense, so I will omit further explanation of this type.

For the purposes of this chapter, we will refer to stress as the suppressive and toxic force that it can be. Stress is the consequence of the body's failure to appropriately respond to emotional or physical threats, whether actual or imagined. Stress can produce a state of alarm, adrenaline and short-term resistance as a survival mechanism, and over time lead to exhaustion and illness. The symptoms, or consequences rather, of stress include emotional irritability, muscular tension, loss of concentration, and a wide variety of physical reactions such as headaches, skin rashes, hair loss, elevated blood pressure, and accelerated heart rate.

> In times of great stress or adversity, it's always best to keep busy, to plow your anger and your energy into something positive.
>
> – *Lee Iacocca*

The most alarming part about stress is that just about anything a human interacts with is a potential stress inducer. From overdue bills, bright lights, traffic, difficult coworkers, death, marriage, divorce, deception, pain, health, and environmental issues such as a lack of control over one's environment like mobility, housing and food to unemployment, insufficient sleep, job pressure, drinking, and adversity can cause stress. I could go on, but you get the picture.

Stress is a toxin that can not only kill your success, but potentially kill you. When I was a sophomore in college, just prior to my Marine Corps unit being activated for Operation Desert Storm, I was taking a time-management and productivity class. I remember the teacher during one of her lessons saying that stress is responsible for more than 80% of the illnesses that a person will experience in their lifetime. I have shared that statistic with others over the years, and many have corrected me with numbers much higher. Whatever the percentage, the experts and laymen alike suggest that stress will be directly or indirectly responsible for almost every illness you will ever have.

For that reason alone, stress must be managed.

There are several ways of coping with stress, such as controlling, limiting, or removing the source of stress. Unfortunately, many stressors can be, and frequently are, essential to our livelihoods. They cannot be avoided, so they must be dealt with.

I am not a doctor, nor am I qualified to counsel anyone on stress management. If stress is a serious concern for you, my advice is to seek professional advice. Fortunately (knock on wood), I have never had to do so. I have been fairly adept at managing my stress, and here is how I do it.

Most of the stress I experience can be grouped into one of two categories:

1. There is something I am avoiding;
2. Subconsciously, I know I am not doing all that I know to do.

I find as soon as I identify my source of stress, and make that first phone call, or send off that first e-mail, or whatever it may be to address the situation, the mere fact that I have identified, addressed, and taken some sort of action toward its resolution dramatically reduces the stress. For me, most stress stems from avoiding something I know I should not be avoiding. As I will share with you later in dealing with another of the five toxins that kill success, I have found that confronting the source is always the best policy.

Toxin #3: Your Thinking

When I refer to your thinking as a toxin, I am speaking of negative thinking and your current thinking (even if it is positive). As the quote reads above, the thinking that got you *here* will not get you *there*. Surely, you have heard Einstein's definition of insanity! It reads, "Insanity is doing the same thing over and over again and expecting a different result." You can easily swap out the word "doing" with "thinking" and the quote's logic would be just as sound.

> We cannot solve our problems with the same thinking we used when we created them.
>
> *— Albert Einstein*

The mind is a fascinating mechanism. When working in a certain way, it will propel you toward and manifest whatever you desire. But the same mind functioning in a different way can produce cataclysmic failure. It all begins with your thoughts:

Bad thoughts = bad results

Good thoughts = good results

Great thoughts = great results

Is it really that simple?

Yes. You become what you think about most of the time.

Negative thinking stems from a selective memory. Most people are inclined to focus on their past disappointments and failures, while rarely recalling their delights and achievements. Regardless of who you are, you have experiences that can be placed in either category, negative and positive. The category you choose to place your focus into most of the time will have a significant impact on your results.

I previously discussed stress and how it is one of the absolutes in life. Discouraging, embarrassing, and frustrating situations will also occur for us all. It is not that successful people experience fewer unpleasant situations than the unsuccessful; it is how the successful people deal with those situations that makes them successful. The two groups respond to unwelcome conditions in entirely different ways.

Unsuccessful people sweat the small stuff. They take the less-than-perfect experiences of life to heart. They dwell, they sulk, and they worry. They focus on the negative. Focusing on the negative creates lasting memories of the negative experience, providing a breeding ground for future negative thoughts, which leads to negative emotions, which causes negative words, which produces negative actions, which creates negative habits, which kindles a negative character. Ultimately one is left with an unfulfilled life.

Conversely, focusing on the positive (as successful people do) produces a fulfilling life. It all begins with your thoughts. Your thoughts need to be monitored closely. At first this sounds like a daunting task, and it can be if you let it. There are hundreds of mind games, techniques, and exercises available to make controlling your thoughts easier. Entire books have been written on this subject alone. Of those books, I recommend *The Science of Success* by James Arthur Ray; *The Answer* by John Assaraf; *Excuse Me, Your Life is Waiting* by Lynn Grabhorn; and of course, *Think and Grow Rich* by Napoleon Hill.

The technique I use to keep my mind filled with positive and productive thoughts was shared with me by my mentor, and it is really simple and effective. Whenever life's circumstances has me down or angry, I command myself to *STOP focusing on what is happening, and START focusing on what I want to have happen*. It works for me every time. Feel free to try it for yourself.

Toxin #4: Guilt

Often it is not the repercussions of wrongdoing that will cause a business to fail, a criminal to be apprehended, or a relationship to end; it is the actions of a guilty conscience. A guilty conscience will cause self-imposed worry, fear, loss of composure, erratic thinking, interrupted concentration, and additional actions that will contribute to and prolong the feeling of guilt.

When you take action or speak words contrary to your conscience, you feel guilt. It is a warning, an internal signal, that you have compromised your own rules for life. Guilt will obstruct your thought process. When your mind is processing thoughts like "Will I get caught? What if they find out? Will I get away with it?", how can any healthy-minded person think straight with such a paranoid and frantic emotion present? There is a saying that when emotions rise, intelligence falls.

A guilt-free life is simple. Operate with honesty and integrity every day of your life and guilt will not be a problem. It is the shortcuts we take in life that lead to guilt. The immediate gratification we experience from such shortcuts is always taken over by worry, erratic thinking, and interrupted concentration. However, should temptation get the best of you one day (and none of us are completely immune), there is a simple five-step process to restore your integrity and rid yourself of guilt:

> Guilt is the source of sorrows, the avenging fiend that follows us behind with whips and stings.
>
> – *Nicholas Rowe*

1. Get in communication with the burdened party.
2. Accept responsibility (do not blame anyone or anything).
3. Acknowledge the impact of your action.
4. Apologize.
5. Volunteer restitution.

Depending on the size of your "short-cut," guilt will generally disappear, or at least begin to. Integrity is restored, and a clear conscience is back intact. You will actually feel a physical relief. That proverbial weight on your shoulders will eventually disappear after implementing the five steps above.

Toxin #5: Indecision

When I got out of the Marine Corps, I remember hearing a quote from General Colin Powell: "Indecision has cost the American government, American businesses, and the American people billions of dollars more than the wrong decision." In other words, NOT making a decision can be more costly than making one, even if it is the wrong one. That quote has stuck with me, and I have referenced it at least a hundred times in conversation since. Making mention of this quote in writing warranted some research in the interest of accuracy.

> There is no more miserable human being than one in whom nothing is habitual but indecision.
>
> – *William James*

It had been so long since I originally heard it, I wanted to make sure I relayed it to you correctly. Funny thing, I was unable to locate the quote worded in the exact same way twice. It appears it has been bastardized significantly over the years, and some sources even gave other people credit for the quote. Nevertheless, it is a compelling notion, and in fact, a notion shared by many. During my fact search, I stumbled across countless esteemed people with a similar, almost identical, belief. Indecision is broadly recognized as a success killer, yet almost completely ignored as a distinction in the world of personal development.

I have divided decisions into two categories.

Category 1 is a "yes" or "no" decision. What will happen if I do? What will happen if I do not?

Category 2 is a "right" or "left" decision. When you find yourself at a fork in the road, you can become paralyzed. Do I turn left? Do I turn right?

The two types have one thing in common. They can stop us dead in our tracks. Through paralysis, relationships deteriorate and businesses fail.

Indecision is toxic. It is the offspring of fear and the mother of paralysis, and it can be costly.

For example, when I was first introduced to my current venture Epic Professionals (www.epicprofessionals.com), I resisted. Not because I was against the idea, but because I was uncertain of how it would work for the average person. After the initial exposure to the opportunity, I thought to myself, "Sounds good, but I'm going to think about it."

In hindsight, this turned out to be a big mistake. The person who had brought the opportunity to my desk decided to move forward with it himself, and in six short months had generated a high-five-figure income and began building a positive cash-flowing real estate portfolio. During this same six-month period, my business had waned significantly. Based on my current success, I estimate that my moment of indecision six months earlier cost me at least $100,000 in actual income and $500,000 in lost opportunity. Had I made the decision to move forward when the opportunity was first presented and then figured out the details later, the most I could've lost was $20,000. I have several examples from the past twenty years of my professional life (and perhaps you do, too) to illustrate the point that indecision is more expensive than making the wrong decision. My ol' pal Theodore Roosevelt agrees (he's not really my pal, we never met☺)...

"In any moment of decision the best thing you can do is the right thing, the next best thing is the wrong thing, and the worst thing you can do is nothing."

– Theodore Roosevelt, 26th President of the United States

Just so we're clear, I'm not suggesting that to be successful you should go out and make a bunch of hasty, uninformed, and irresponsible decisions. Well… almost. What I'm suggesting, is don't use the "Let me think about it" answer as an excuse to not make a decision. Do think about it, do some research, but then *decide*. Decide swiftly, and here's why. Decision causes movement, and nothing happens without a decision. The danger with "nothing happening" is you are unknowingly moving backwards. You are not just standing still while waiting to make the right decision, you are moving backwards because life continues to move forward. If you find yourself paralyzed by indecision, life will pass you by.

"Life is short" is an old saying, but I've come to know it better as "Life is fast," and the older you get the faster it seemingly gets. In our rapidly evolving times, my experience has led me to believe we no longer live in a world where the strong pummel the weak or the big swallow the small.

We now live in a world where the fast overtake the slow.

Brian Tracy, an expert and author of multiple books on leadership, sales, management, and business strategy, cites two principles of his *21 Success Secrets of Self-Made Millionaires* dealing with decisions and the speed in which we make them. Develop a reputation for speed and

> Whenever you see a successful business, someone once made a courageous decision.
>
> *– Peter F. Drucker, Writer, Father of "Modern Management"*

dependability (Principle #13), and be decisive and action oriented (Principle #19).

A while back a very good friend of mine called me on the phone raving about a little town in Alabama where we could pick up small houses for $3,500. My friend went on and on about how he was witnessing with his own eyes the transformation of this little town, and one specific street in particular.

"Matt, I already bought one house and I'm going to buy another very soon. You should at least pick up one for yourself. This town's value is going to explode! It's so obvious (citing many positive economic factors)," he shared with enthusiasm.

I got off the phone very excited, yet depression soon set in when reality hit me that I only had $5,000 to my name and rent was due. I shared my situation with a few friends and to my surprise a couple of them offered to loan me the money to do it.

"Really?" was my initial delighted response, and then I followed it up with, "Let me think about it."

To make a long story short, I never took my friends up on their generous and gracious offers. Six months later, property values had soared to $30,000, and a couple of years later to $75,000. Even as the nation's real estate values took a significant hit in 2008, that little street was virtually unaffected as the value of that real estate today is sitting at $100,000, give or take a few thousand. By not making that decision to accept the gesture of $3,500 offered by my friends, I lost a minimum of $70,000 and the opportunity to give back a sizeable return to my friends who were willing to loan me the money.

Had I accepted their offers, made the investment, and the

> There are only two options regarding commitment. You're either in or out. There's no such thing as a life in-between.
>
> – Pat Riley, World Champion Basketball Coach

opportunity failed to pan out, I would've lost a mere $3,500. In hindsight, it would've only taken me a few months to recover and pay back my friends. Decisions are important, and their impact on one's life can be grossly ignored. As described above, it can be the smallest decisions that can change a life.

The subsequent three years turned out to be the worst for me financially than the previous fifteen. Had I made a decision to join my friend in pursuing investments in that neighborhood, the impact of an extra $50,000, $100,000, or $200,000 during those years could've opened up many other opportunities.

Napoleon Hill, in his classic _Think and Grow Rich_, notes a distinction between the rich and the poor in the speed with which they make decisions. The rich make up their minds quickly and change them slowly, while the poor make up their minds slowly and change them quickly. These are words coming from a man who has associated with, and interviewed more, wealthy people (the wealthiest!) than anyone probably ever will. The effects of mistakes caused by my wrong decisions have been no greater than the effects of my extended vacillation, my "thinking about it." Decide, and do it quickly.

If all you had to do was start making quicker decisions to mitigate the effects of an indecisive way of living, would you do it? I am coming to know that a prosperous, enlivened, and productive life is yours for the taking by simply making decisions and making them quickly. I am struggling less and less with the question, "Is it that simple?" Actually, yes it has been. Easy? It can be with a little

> If you chase two rabbits, both will escape.
>
> – _Chinese Proverb_

discipline and practice. It's getting easier and easier, and now, having it as a distinction, it's becoming a very useful tool.

Each time I (and I invite you to consider this) put off making a decision, I rob myself of time and a clear mind, resulting in lost days and performance. To compound the problem, more days are lost lamenting over those lost days!

But the true cost of indecision is not limited to wasted time and lost opportunity. Indecision exacerbates worry and breeds heartache and sadness. Indecision can be debilitating. It can take on a life of its own and creep into your character. It can be contagious and infect others. It can chip away at your self-confidence and the confidence others have in you. It will not only stifle your progress, it will stifle that of the people around you.

So, here it is. Whether you think you can or cannot do, just *begin*. Just do it, if you will. Perhaps "indecision" was the inspiration for the Nike slogan? Just do the best you know how at the moment of decision. As you do, more times than not you will come to realize that it is not always what we know or have analyzed prior to making a decision that makes it a good one, it is what we do *after* the decision that makes it good.

When the time comes, and it always does, that you are faced with two evenly balanced courses of action, choose the bolder. Always choose the bolder. When making a bold decision, unseen forces come to your aid. The path to producing bold results is making bold decisions, and in boldness there is power and genius. People give their hearts, their loyalty and their business to power and genius. General George S. Patton once said that the willingness to make decisions is the most important quality in a good leader. He also said a good plan today is better than a perfect plan tomorrow.

At the end of each day I block out thirty minutes to plan the following day. In the middle of my planning process, I ask myself, "Is there anything today that I left undecided?" Whatever is left undecided goes on the "to-do" list for tomorrow. I schedule the time for the following day in which I am going to make the decision and to whom I am going to communicate it to. This single discipline has liberated me from most of my worries and uncertainty, and in addition to keeping my life moving forward, I sleep much better.

Toxin #6: Fear

Fear! What is it? I mean really, what is it? Literally, it is a distressing emotion aroused by impending danger, evil, or pain. Fear is a basic survival mechanism related to the behaviors of fight, flee, escape, or avoidance. The capacity to fear is a part of human nature. This emotion is both learned and inherited; it is a lesson that has been passed on from generation to generation beginning millions of years ago when humans initially learned to fear the likes of saber-toothed tigers and hungry wolves (now that's what I call impending danger, evil, or pain!). The last I checked, threat from these beasts did not interfere with my last attempt at success. How about yours? Probably not, but everyday fears that seem just as strong still exist. What is important to get is that the vast majority (I feel comfortable going on the record with 99.9%) of fears we face *cannot* be categorized as impending danger, evil, or pain. There are few things out there that will kill us or cause us physical harm. As long as we look both ways when crossing the street and steer away from dark alleys at night, most danger, evil, and pain can be virtually eliminated from a person's life. Then why does fear still stop us? The answer is simple. Whether a threat is real or imagined, the mind will not automatically make the distinction. The mind will initially categorize everything as a saber-toothed tiger.

> I learned that courage was not the absence of fear, but the triumph over it. The brave man is not he who does not feel afraid, but he who conquers that fear.
>
> *– Nelson Mandela*

Most fear we experience today is strictly psychological. This makes many people wonder if there is any truth to the F.E.A.R. acronym: False Evidence Appearing Real. This acronym has been used so much that it has lost its punch. As with so many clichés and idioms, overuse decreases their impact and exhausts their value and benefit. The cynics have dismissed F.E.A.R. as a "self-help" manipulation tool, something used to influence people to spend money on books and videos and workshops.

Let's not dismiss the F.E.A.R. acronym, though. There is an invaluable lesson to learn here. Fear really is false evidence within the mind that has been created by the mind and then projected into reality and into one's future. And when this takes place, people get stopped dead in their tracks and live unfulfilling lives of boundaries and limits. A life of limits is a life of restrictions on achievement, and that is precisely how fear keeps us from realizing our goals.

Simply knowing this, unfortunately, is not enough to manage fear. The vacuous encouragement from the crowd "it's only in your mind" presumes that fear is not real. But it is. Fear is real. Fear is the number one killer of success. Fear will stop you from seizing opportunity. It will steal your energy, it will make you sick, it will cause stress, and in my opinion fear's most crippling (and costly) effect is that fear will clamp your mouth shut when you want to speak.

Fear, for our context, is synonymous with uncertainty, unfamiliarity, and lack of (or the absence of) confidence, which leads to paralysis. It is why millions of people accomplish little, achieve little, experience little, and enjoy little. Fear is a powerfully suppressive force. Directly, or indirectly, fear is responsible for people "wanting" most of their lives. In my opinion, fear is tantamount to a psychological infection. Fortunately, we can cure such an infection in the same way we cure a physical infection. Once diagnosed, a proven treatment can be prescribed.

Before I prescribe the procedure to cure the "fear infection," however, you will need to be prepped for surgery (metaphorically speaking; no sharp instruments will be used). As fear is learned, it can be unlearned. You will want to adopt the belief that certainty, familiarity, and confidence are learned, acquired, and developed. Like your biceps, confidence is also a muscle. As there are exercises to develop your biceps, there are exercises to develop your confidence. In order to keep your biceps in shape, ongoing exercise is necessary. The same is true to keep your confidence in shape.

Gratitude

Your first exercise is to practice an attitude of gratitude. It is impossible for gratitude and fear to simultaneously exist. Be grateful. A daily ritual I recommend is spending 10, 20, or even 30 minutes counting your blessings. Start by being grateful for the things closest to you, such as a healthy heart, and move out to things more distant. I typically do this during my morning workout.

The conversation in my head sounds something like this: "I am grateful for my healthy heart. I am grateful for my healthy lungs. I am grateful for my arms and legs. I am grateful for my able body. I am grateful that I get to exercise every morning in a beautiful place like Southern California. I am grateful for my family. I am grateful I get to go to work every day doing what I love, and so on…" I really get into it. I make sure I am really feeling, I mean FEELING, gratitude. This works. Do not underestimate the power and positive impact this exercise will have over fear, not to mention your overall mindset and thinking.

Action

Your second exercise is to get into action. Fear is easily managed by taking action. Action quickly builds confidence. Conversely, inaction will increase fear and destroy confidence. On a daily basis do that thing you fear most, and do it first, and fear will disappear. Your life can be completely transformed by heeding this one tiny bit of advice. You will be amazed how liberating this practice can be. Not only does it clear your mind of worry and guilt, it clears your mind for the rest of the day. And a clear mind communicates better, thinks more creatively and sleeps in peace. A well-rested, creative person who communicates clearly and often, produces results…successful results.

Are you one for extra credit? Are you one for immediate gratification? Nothing, nothing that I have been exposed to in the last twenty years of my professional life, eradicates fear and builds confidence with more velocity than this exercise. If you choose to take this on, from this day forward, every time (and I mean every time) you are afraid of something, you must face it. For this exercise to be as effective as I suggested above, it is paramount that you are aware that fear does not always show up as fear. Fear stops us daily, disguised as procrastination, reluctance, discouragement, aversion, apathy, hostility and indifference. In one year, by implementing this rule, my self-confidence has grown more than it did in the previous ten.

So that you are now clear how this exercise looks, here are some basic examples:

- Imagine you are afraid to call that special someone to ask for a date. *You call, now!*
- Imagine you have been procrastinating following up with your last business appointment. *You follow up, now!*
- Imagine you have been dodging a bill collector's call. *You call them back, now!*
- Imagine the boss just asked you to give a presentation to the board of directors. *You accept, immediately!*

Initially, this exercise is challenging. Perhaps just the thought of this exercise already terrifies you. If that's the case, you know what you have to do to conquer this fear. *Implement it, now!* My business partner J. comments repeatedly how he lives in "now o'clock," and because he does, his confidence increases by the day and he produces great results.

Your mind will eventually begin to trust that nowhere out there is a saber-toothed tiger waiting to eat you, and the exercise will get easier. It may be unfathomable to you at this point, but you will begin to really enjoy the exercise. I promise, and here is why. What awaits you on the other side of your fears is a liberating and powerful life of exhilaration and joy; and according to the Law of Being, you will begin to have what a person who confronts their fears has: results, achievement and success. You will experience results you have never experienced before because you are now doing something you have never consistently done before – confronting your fears.

Like the building of the bicep I mentioned before, it takes work and it takes time. Your confidence muscle will get stronger with work and time, as well. If you continue to work it, your confidence muscle will grow. You will begin to associate fear with results, and what was once debilitating now calls you powerfully into action. Your journey to success begins to accelerate, and contrary to what your intuition might lead you to believe, the faster the journey moves, the easier it gets.

Now isn't this exciting? It's so exciting that later I will dedicate an entire chapter of this book to fear and share with you how it can be your most powerful ally on your road to success.

Toxin #7: Environment and People

Does that quote from H. Clement Stone cause you to immediately think of your environment, like it did me? Now knowing that you will become your friends, does it cause you to immediately think of your friends? Do you want to become your friends?

I have often thought, and perhaps you have thought something similar, what would my life be like if I would have been born in a different country? Would I be a fan of the same music? Would my favorite foods be the same? Which football team would I root for? Would I even like football? What would I be doing for a living? It is impossible to know for certain, but at the same time there is

> Be careful the environment you choose for it will shape you; be careful the friends you choose for you will become like them.
>
> – *H. Clement Stone*

certainty that I would be different, as would you being raised in a different environment than what you were. Depending on the environment, it is not farfetched to suggest we would be significantly different. The human condition has a propensity to assimilate to its environment. Who you are and who you will become is greatly influenced by your environment.

The way you talk, your choice of entertainment, your style of dress and all of your other idiosyncrasies were given to you by another person or your environment. Not totally convinced? Name one habit, trait or mannerism that is 100% yours. Try to name one that was not given to you or inspired by another. The point is, choose your environment carefully. If who you are now is because of where you have been, then who you will become will be considerably determined by your future environment.

Early in my *Do Over*, empowered with this distinction, I made a conscious decision to change my environment. My current environment wasn't working for me. I felt uninspired and unproductive working from home. In fact, I got lazy and just the thought of getting dressed, leaving the house and meeting new clients became exhausting. Keeping myself motivated was a serious concern. All it took were a couple of "no's" from new prospects to ruin my day; and if those "no's" happened in the morning, the afternoon was shot. I wasn't stretching myself, nor was I being stretched by my environment. Growth seemed to have ceased completely. My attitude was deteriorating, and the size of my dreams dwindled from "grand possibility" to "mere survival." I could go on about how bad my thinking had gotten, but you get the point.

After weighing my options for environments, I chose boldly. I chose an environment of young, energetic, goal-oriented doers fifty miles away. The commute from my bedroom to the downstairs office transformed overnight to a daily two-hour roundtrip. My monthly gasoline bill and office expenses tripled. My much-coveted eight-hours-a-night sleep had to be sacrificed, but it was worth it. It was worth, and still is worth, every extra minute and every penny. Since the move, my dreams have been restored, skills strengthened, activity increased, results multiplied, and confidence bolstered. I give every ounce of credit to my decision to change my environment.

The way you think, your attitudes, the size of your dreams and goals, and your very personality will be shaped, if not completely altered, by your environment. Experts and independent studies agree that a person consistently functioning in an environment of negative thinkers, petty attitudes, and pessimistic dispositions will take on those traits. Not to worry; by surrounding yourself with ambitious people you will increase your ambition. Continued companionship with big thinkers will increase your thinking. Prosperous camaraderie will contribute to your prosperity.

The Thinking Around Us

Regardless of what we are up to, and more than we are aware, the thinking around us dictates who we are. Unfortunately, most of this thinking is small. We are constantly surrounded by an environment that is tugging at us. The metaphor for this I hear frequently is that of a "bucket of crabs." I have never been crabbing, but it goes something like this. If you were to put a crab into a bucket, you would have to place a lid on the bucket in order to keep the crab from crawling out. Once you have placed a second crab in the bucket, the lid is no longer necessary. The reason being is as soon as one crab attempts its escape, the other crab will pull it back into the bucket.

Who are the crabs in your life?

Do you regularly hear expressions like "a bird in the hand beats two in the bush," "curiosity killed the cat," and "there are too many chiefs and not enough Indians?" In other words, your environment is telling you to be happy with what you have, that being inquisitive will kill you and there's no more room at the top. An environment of "crabs" will insist it's too crowded and there is too much competition for the top spots in life. Is that true? If your answer is yes, or your answer is no, Henry Ford would tell you that you are correct. Your answer to that question is also a clue to your current environment.

A family friend who employs thousands once told me he receives fifty times as many job applications for the positions that pay $50,000 and lower than for the jobs that pay $100,000 and above. That clearly demonstrates where the competition is, doesn't it? Not only is there less competition at the top, the people are nicer, the resources are more abundant, the air is cleaner and the views are better. Most importantly, the thinking is bigger; and if great minds think alike, surround yourself with great minds and big thinkers.

The Right People

Regardless if your next endeavor is to be an entrepreneur, an actor, a politician, a doctor, chairman of a non-profit, vice president of your company, or whatever your pursuit may be, on your way up you will be interacting with other people. Vendors, customers, directors, producers, investors, managers, patients, colleagues, family, friends, superiors, subordinates, mentors, and critics will need to be incorporated into your plan if success is to be yours. Surrounding yourself with the right people is paramount.

Principle #17 of Brian Tracy's *21 Success Secrets of Self-Made Millionaires* is "Get around the right people." Relationships are everything! Tracy goes on to say that 85% of your success in life will be determined by both your personal and business relationships. I'm not sure how one would go about determining a statistic like that, but based on my experience 85% is conservative.

On the road to success, there are two types of people you will want to steer clear of or dramatically limit your association with:

1. Those who are afraid to travel the road themselves, and
2. Those who are afraid you will make it.

It is not surprising, but it is certainly disappointing, that many of your close friends and family members will fall into one of these two categories. I created an exercise to help you identify the toxic people in your life. I will later give you my recommendation of what to do once they are identified, but it is up to you how you associate with them from this point forward.

Take a sheet of paper and make a list of all the people you are certain to interact with over the next twelve months. On a separate piece of paper, draw a line down the middle so you have two columns. On the left side, title the column "People who poison me," and on the right side "People who love me, but also poison me."

PEOPLE WHO POISON ME	PEOPLE WHO LOVE ME BUT ALSO POISON ME

Now, go through that original list one name at a time and imagine yourself sharing with that person that you were going into business for yourself. What is their most likely response? If you imagine that person laughing at you or calling you crazy, write their name on the left hand side of the paper. If you imagine that person empathetically trying to talk you out of it, write their name on the right hand side of the paper. If you imagine the person being inquisitive or supportive, you will not write their name on either side.

Once you have sorted every name on the list, you get to make a decision. Whatever you decide is entirely up to you, but this is what I did:

1. I eliminated *all contact* with the people in the left column, the poisonous people. These people are no longer in my life.
2. I eliminated *all conversation about my goals* with the people on the right, the people who love me. I love them too, and I enjoy their company. I simply change the subject if my ambitions come up in conversation, politely of course.

Again, what you do with the people on the list is entirely up to you, but that's what I did. You know your situation better than I do.

Here is another perspective. If you told a millionaire you were determined to make a million dollars in the next twelve months, the last thing they would do is laugh or suggest you were crazy. In fact, that millionaire might offer some advice on how to make it happen, or how they might help. That's a hint about what your new environment should include, by the way.

Your environment is important. Your environment will be a source of stress, an influence on your thoughts, a sway of discerning right from wrong, and a support when faced with challenges. At the end of the day, if you do not create the right environment and have the right people around you, the repercussions can be swift and severe. A toxic environment and toxic people will not just slow you down, they will lead you down dead-end paths.

You are a product of your environment, and you will become a product of the environment you create. If you create an environment of losers, you will lose. If you create an environment of achievers, you will achieve. The bright side is YOU get to create your environment.

CHAPTER 3:
LIVING IN THE BOX

"A person starts to live when he can live outside himself."

– Albert Einstein

Up to this point I have suggested *Your Relationship to Success* and *The Seven Toxins that Kill Success* as inquiries to help reveal some of your invisible barriers. Most people by now will have already noticed some, maybe several, missteps they made in previous endeavors. For example, through these inquiries you might have identified and written down that you previously felt undeserving of success, and as a result have unknowingly sabotaged yourself; or you have made note that your "being" was correlated with that of a victim or a cynic; or you have been able to clearly distinguish sources of stress, your own unproductive thoughts, the harboring of guilt, habits of indecision, unwarranted fear, or a toxic environment.

Most people I coach will have pages full of notes thus far. Or, sometimes nothing has been revealed yet, and that is okay, too. The next two chapters will reveal two invisible barriers that are common to every human being. If you're human, you have them. And if you don't know what they are and how to deal with them, they will likely keep whatever you are seeking in life forever beyond your grasp.

The Box

As humans, we have one specific system and one specific condition in common. In this chapter we will explore the innate system called your survival system. Or, what I like to refer to as your "box." Growing up, we all unknowingly created a box that we live within. The purpose of this box is to protect us from everything that exists outside the box. It automatically distinguishes for us the difference between "right and wrong" and "good and bad." The box is so efficient in defending us through these distinctions that most people will never know of its existence. But make no mistake, it's there, and it's very powerful. It pretty much governs everything you do. Nope...not pretty much everything...everything! I mentioned earlier the expression, "How you do one thing is how you do everything." It is from this proverbial box that this expression originates.

The box is an automated defense system similar to what we refer to as reflexes. Just as you automatically pull your hand away from fire, the box will automatically protect you from responsibility or commitment. Just as your eyelid will automatically close (or blink) when something quickly approaches your eye, the box will automatically protect you from embarrassment or looking bad. In a nutshell, the box protects your ego. Maybe you're thinking, "What's wrong with that? That doesn't sound so bad to me."

Here's the rub. The box that protects your ego also impedes your living a fulfilling life. In other words, everything you want that you don't have exists outside your box, and the box won't let it in. This idea may be intriguing to some, confusing to others, and outlandish to the rest. Whatever category you are in, remember our sunglasses analogy. We're just trying them on. If they don't fit, we're putting them back on the rack.

Every human has his or her own box, yet each box varies greatly from human to human. In fact, no two boxes are quite the same size or shape. The box *gives us* each our own unique identity, our character and personality, and with that comes our self-imposed limitations. Our awareness of how we live with, and how we work in and out of, the box is what will make the difference in the achievement of our goals. I'll go into that more later, because before we can work with the box we will need to identify how we each created our own unique version.

Okay, enough with the cryptic talk. Although some of you may be following along with no problem, I'm guessing a great number of you could be completely lost. What in the world is this box? For those of you with that question, and to clarify for those of you who think you're right there with me, I'll give you a real life example.

Imagine someone were to spit in your face. By the very nature of being human, an automatic response would be stimulated. But what would that response be? Can you agree that different people would respond in different ways? Meaning, one person may reciprocate and spit back, another may break down and cry in embarrassment, another may respond with a right hook, and another may turn the other cheek and simply walk away. This is a rather extreme, and crude, example, but it illustrates the point very effectively.

Three Employees

Here's a more practical example to demonstrate how the box can directly affect your success. Imagine three warehouse employees of a widget manufacturing plant. Each employee feels they are underpaid, and each has overdue bills. All three are unsatisfied with their jobs and do nothing but complain during breaks and lunch about their respective situations. One day the department manager calls the three into a meeting and presents to them an opportunity to participate in a percentage of the company's monthly profits by making cold calls to solicit new business. Each employee will receive a bonus in direct proportion to the new business they generate in addition to their current paycheck.

Employee #1

Responds with enthusiasm, making one hundred calls resulting in increased business for the company and a generous bonus for himself. Employee #1's bills are paid, and he or she receives a promotion for their outstanding work.

Employee #2

Responds with reluctance, makes a few calls and then quits, resulting in a nominal bonus. He's still behind on his bills and maintains his current position.

Employee #3

Is paralyzed by the fear of calling strangers and makes no calls, resulting in nothing. In result, employee #3 is now on the short list to be laid off during the next downsizing.

A less enlightened observer might call employee #1 "ambitious," employee #2 your "average Joe," and employee #3 "lazy." I want you to resist taking this common and obvious position and consider it has nothing to do with ambition or laziness and everything to do with their respective boxes. Each employee has been hardwired to respond. Their survival system is protecting them from being wrong or looking bad. That's what the box does. To clarify, employee #1's definition of looking bad was not paying his bills, so he took advantage of the opportunity he was given. Employee #3's definition of looking bad was imposing on prospective customers via unsolicited calls, so he made no calls. Employee #2 waffled in between, gave it a try and likely received a few disgruntled responses from his calls, and quit. Each employee was given equal opportunity, yet each responded differently. These three employees had a choice in how to respond to the department manager's proposal, but rarely do people consciously choose. The box typically chooses for them. It's automatic.

Hopefully, you now have some insight as to how this box may impede your efforts and results. What I want to draw your attention to right now is how a human gets hardwired, and how this box gets created. Identifying how your box was created is the first step to living outside of it.

I have been taught about the box from several sources, all of whom have put their own twist on the concept and assigned it their own unique name. I have implemented the lessons I have learned and can firsthand confirm the box's existence and power. Based on my lessons and life experience, however, I have come up with my own theory on how it works. As with the Law of Being and the Law of Gravity, it's not as important to understand how it works, but to understand that it exists. Nevertheless, I have a theory on the inner workings of how we each create our box.

Your Reticular Activating System

The part of the brain known as the reticular activating system (RAS) is responsible for the box's creation. The RAS is the name given to the part of the brain believed to be the center of awareness, arousal, and motivation. The activity of this system is crucial for maintaining a state of consciousness. Its proper function is a prerequisite for consciousness and awareness to occur.

I remember during the summer after I graduated from high school, the transmission of my old Nissan 200SX Turbo went *kaput*. My mom, bless her heart, was there to save the day (again) and ponied up for a new transmission. $3,500 later the car soon blew a gasket for something like the sixth time in two years at $300 a pop.

It was time to get rid of this maintenance-plagued money pit and get a new car. My mom and I drove to the Nissan dealership to have a look around, and when I laid my eyes on the brand new version of my car, the 240SX, I just about lost it. The car was beautiful! I wanted it so badly I couldn't contain myself. I could vividly imagine myself driving down the street being the first one on the block with this beauty.

The dealer was generous with my trade-in, a transaction was conducted, and off I went in my brand-new 240SX. Not ten minutes on the road with my new wheels I had pulled up to a stoplight right beside another 240SX. That's odd; I had never seen this car before tonight and within ten minutes there another one was. Oh well, moving on... Before I had got the car home I had seen another, and within a week I had noticed at least a dozen Nissan 240SXs.

What does this story have to do with the RAS? It has everything to do with the RAS, and everything to do with the creation of your box.

You see, the day before I purchased that new 240SX I had no awareness of the 240SX. Once I purchased the car and owned it myself, my RAS had been activated. My awareness of the car had been switched on, and the car seemed to appear around every corner. That is how the RAS works, and that is precisely how the RAS creates your box.

As humans, we are the only creatures on earth that are born into a natural state of disorientation with the world. As opposed to other creatures that are guided by instinct, we have been given the power to create our lives. Whether we are aware of it or not, each and every one of us does exactly that every day. We form thoughts, speak words, make decisions and take actions on a daily basis that endlessly shape our lives. We come into this world self-expressed and absent of inhibitions. This condition lasts until somewhere between the age of three or five years, when we are confronted with our first pivotal decision. I refer to these as "pivotal" decisions because in these moments of decision, and they happen in an instant, your life is hardwired by these decisions. With this first decision, the first of four pillars of your survival system is put in place. Your box has been placed and is taking shape. Your RAS has been activated.

Pivotal Decisions

This first pivotal decision to which I'm referring is the very first time in your life you recognized something here isn't quite right. It's the very first time your free and fun-loving life, a life without a care in the world, gets rocked. It was in that moment you made your first pivotal decision, you decided who you were going to be and how you would forever adapt when faced with a situation of "something's not quite right."

After learning of these pivotal decisions of life, it took almost a year before I was able to uncover mine, I remember I was three or four years old and my mother had just remarried. I don't remember a whole lot from that time. I can't even place the house where this happened. What I do remember is the night of the wedding my mother and new stepfather were fighting like cats and dogs, and it seemed they fought all night. I was in my bedroom with the door closed with my head under the pillow. I was unable to discern the content of the argument; all I remember was loud yelling – lots of yelling.

That wasn't when I made my first pivotal decision, however. The decision came early the next morning, after peace had seemingly been restored. I opened my bedroom door, walked out, and on my way to the stairs I had noticed on the ground the aftermath of the night before. I saw the hat that my mother had worn in her wedding torn to shreds. It was in that moment I decided "something's not quite right." In that moment I could've decided to be an abuser, a protector, or a caregiver. There are a number of choices I could've made. In that moment I became an over-accommodating individual who avoids confrontation. The hat that had been torn to shreds represented the hurt feelings of my mother and the effects of loud confrontation. My RAS had been activated; my box had taken its initial shape.

Once this initial shape has been taken, the RAS will from that point forward focus on evidence that proves the box correct, bolstering the strength of the box. Not only will the RAS continue to notice evidence confirming the box, it will actually seek out evidence to strengthen the box. This first decision, and the other three to follow, have pervaded my entire life (as your pivotal decisions pervade yours).

Whenever I am faced with confrontation, whether in personal or business matters, my box wants to keep the peace. This box has placed a limit on the amount of confrontation it will allow me to endure, even if persistence in the matter would serve me. The box remembers my mother's hurt feelings and shredded hat. The box doesn't want to relive that moment, or any moment that may cause the same results (literally and figuratively). It's so powerful in its duty of keeping the peace, it will cause a "confrontation adverse" person like myself to violently avoid a threat to restore the peace.

I am an accommodating individual even when not faced with confrontation. This pillar of my box makes me a naturally good host at dinner parties, a chivalrous man, one always willing to allow another car the right of way. These characteristics of my life are on autopilot. It's simply how my survival system works. It's hardwired, and it is what it is. There are ways in which the box serves me, and there are ways in which it doesn't. It stifles my self-expression, and it causes me to clam up when speaking my mind would benefit me and others. Here's the good news: I am now aware of how it doesn't serve me. I am conscious of its existence and impact, and it is then and only then that one can begin to take control of this automated response.

Some will instantly remember their first moment of "something's not quite right," others will have to inquire for a while before they get it, and the rest of you may never remember – and that's okay. What's important is that you know it happened. If you don't remember and you're dying to know, contact me through the contact form on my website, http://thedooverguy.com/. Perhaps we can work through it together?

Realization: I Suck!

We're not done. There are three other pivotal decisions we all will make in our lives. The second pivotal decision reveals itself somewhere in grammar school, first to sixth grade. It is the moment in which you decide you don't stack up. It typically happens the first time you compare yourself to someone else or you fail to meet expectations (yours or someone else's). The words you utter at this moment are not actually that polite, however. In this moment you actually say to yourself, "I suck." Maybe your exact word isn't "suck," but you get the picture. It can be the first time you were picked last for the kickball team, or lost the spelling bee, or were scolded by a teacher for a bad paper, or were laughed at for the clothes you wore, the way you talk, the way you look, or for so many people, the first time you're rejected by the opposite sex.

A woman once shared with me that when she was a little girl she spent a summer vacation with her grandparents. When she returned home there was a new baby in the house. Her mother had given birth to a new daughter, and the girl's first thought was, "Who is this? Why do you need another child when you have me? Am I not good enough?" To demonstrate that she was good enough and *didn't suck*, in an instant she decided to be an overachiever. There's no doubt in my mind that this was the case because at the time she shared this with me, this woman had two Ph.D.s, managed her own practice, chaired the board of two different hospitals, was president of her son's PTA, volunteered for three different non-profits, and competed in triathlons. I'm tired just writing about it. Again, here's the rub…her marriage was on the rocks, and her son was constantly in trouble at school and with the law. Her box was working overtime to prove she was good enough. Her box made no time for her family where she likely felt she was good enough through the expressions of her family's love. She took her family for granted.

Here's what you deserve to start seeing…if your box is controlling your life, it will generally leave you unfulfilled. One's box may produce poverty, yet fulfilling relationships. Another's may produce riches, yet the inability to relax. If the box is what's producing the positive aspects of your life, it's also creating the negative aspects.

I Don't Belong

We now have a box that was originally created by "something's not quite right," and then reduced in size after deciding "I suck." It then gets a little smaller after the third pivotal decision. This is the moment in life where you first realize you're different, or you don't belong. This moment is closely related to the "I suck" moment a few years earlier, but this moment is distinct. The RAS has been able to acquire enough evidence that you're not good enough that one day comes and it smacks you upside the head with, "You flat-out just don't belong!" Typically, and not surprisingly, this happens sometime in high school. It can be the moment you're excluded from the "cool" crowd, or maybe the first time you realize there even is a cool crowd and you're not in it. As with the previous pivotal decisions, this moment can occur in a wide variety of situations, but I'm confident you get the gist of "I don't belong." At this third pivotal decision, we're old enough that recalling this one is fairly quick, easy and obvious.

I remembered mine vividly. During my freshman year in high school, the break dancing craze was picking up steam on the West Coast. I was fascinated the first time I saw it. I loved the dancing, the music and the clothes – oh, the parachute pants! Being a Caucasian kid going to school in upper middle-class Irvine, California in 1983, there weren't too many at my school who shared my newly found passion.

Here's an image for you...imagine a Southern California high school in 1983 where the girls either looked like Madonna, Pat Benatar, Cyndi Lauper, or Molly Ringwald; the guys with their feathered hair, "Risky Business" Ray-Bans and stonewashed jeans; the music of The Police, The Talking Heads, The Cure and "The Boss" blaring out of the Volkswagen Rabbits, Jettas, and Siroccos; Rubik's Cubes, crimped hair, Swatches, rubber bracelets, sweaters around the waist, rolled sleeves, leg

> **The irony is by trying to appear authentic, the exact opposite is produced: inauthenticity.**
>
> *– Matt Theriault*

warmers, spandex...you get the picture. It was the '80s! If you're too young and these words are not bringing up vivid imagery for you, the movies *Sixteen Candles* or *Can't Buy Me Love* make great reference material. Now, imagine a 4'11" skinny Caucasian kid wearing an oversized hooded Nike windbreaker, bright yellow baggy pants with zippers down the side and sporting some white

Converse Chuck Taylor high-tops with fat red laces, walking through the lunch area, completely oblivious to how out of place he looked. Yep, that was me. I was into it all: break dancing and rap music was my thing. I lived and breathed everything Herbie Hancock, Run D.M.C., Grandmaster Flash, and hip-hop.

I remember one day in the locker room after P.E. as I was sliding on my yellow baggy pants. From over my shoulder I heard a sneering voice utter just one word: "Poser." Laughter erupted! That's all it took. In my world, that was the worst thing to be called. Hip-hop is all about being authentic, being true to the game, living the culture, surviving adversity, and fighting the man. Looking back, it's hilarious that I was able to create that world for myself in Irvine (birthplace of the "yuppie"), but I did. It was very real to me. I was devastated by the utterance of this one word. I had just been informed that I didn't belong to my school's crowd, nor did I belong to the hip-hop crowd either. My box shrunk yet again.

It was in that moment I decided I would never be called a "poser" again, and from that day forward I would go the extra mile in everything I did to appear authentic. Being authentic now represented belonging to me.

The irony is by trying to *appear* authentic, the exact opposite is produced: inauthenticity. That is how my box adapts to "I don't belong." Study, study, study…analyze, analyze, analyze…process, process, process…make sure you know everything before taking on any endeavor. Although preparation is a strength of mine that serves me very well in many arenas, it limits me in others, as I'm inclined to "get ready to get ready" or be stopped by "analysis paralysis." I'm wired that way, it's the third dimension of my box, and it's okay. It's okay because I'm aware that it's there and I know how it impacts me and those around me; and because of that awareness I can control it. For example, the awareness of this dimension is what has allowed this book to leave my perpetual editing hands so you could actually acquire it.

There is amazing power in this awareness of how my box wants to protect me by slowly thinking things through, over-preparing, overanalyzing, and over-processing. I can look back on my life and clearly see the toll this dimension of my box has taken. Now, when I recognize this dimension taking over, I consciously implement the "ready, fire, aim" strategy to achievement. In other words, when I find myself stopped by overanalyzing, I recognize it, make a decision and proceed. More often than not it produces a favorable result, sometimes not what I had intended to produce, but favorable, nonetheless.

I Am On My Own

The last pivotal decision, the final shaping of your box, will generally happen somewhere in early adulthood. It's the moment you first realize that "it's all up to you." You will say something to the effect that "I am on my own." At that moment, just like the previous three moments, you make a decision to be a certain way whenever you find yourself faced with "I am on my own."

A good friend of mine, whom I will call "Joel," remembers this pivotal decision vividly. It was a few months after he had graduated from college, and he had decided to remain living near the campus. To help Joel get on his feet, Joel's dad moved him into an apartment while Joel searched for a job. Joel searched half-heartedly because his father was subsidizing his cost of living with a monthly allowance. Joel felt no sense of urgency to become employed.

A few months passed, and reality was settling in. Life after college was turning out to be more challenging than Joel had expected. After about four months of this "job searching" and living off of Dad's dime, Joel called home requesting some additional financial assistance. For the first time in his life, Joel's dad declined his request. "It's time you stood on your own two feet," Joel's dad said, and he meant it.

Living far from home, it was in that moment Joel realized for the very first time he was on his own. He was terrified. In that moment, he forever decided to be resourceful in the face of *I am on my own*. Now, that doesn't sound like a bad thing to be, and it's not. The flipside of that coin, however, is Joel is extremely controlling. He must do everything himself and has issues with delegating. This one dimension, as Joel tells it, is responsible for three different business ventures failing. He admits he is great at getting the businesses up and running (because his box is resourceful), yet when it comes time to hire help, he micromanages (because his box won't let him delegate) every employee right out the door.

When Joel finally got down to the source of his failures, once he was able to define the four dimensions of his box (particularly the fourth), he is now able to recognize it when it gets in the way. He trusts his "resourceful" box to find the right employees and then lets go and allows them to do what he hired them to do. Sure, it's a struggle for him, and he occasionally slips back into his micromanaging ways, but when challenges occur on the job, Joel knows precisely where to look first. "Am I micromanaging?" he asks himself. If the answer is yes, he lets go. If the answer is no, he inquires within the other three dimensions of the box.

Hopefully, it is becoming clear how awareness of your box gives you power. Who you are, what you do, and what you have right now resides inside your box. Who you want to be, what you want to do, and what you want to have in life resides outside the box. So, if you are to achieve what you want, what you don't currently possess, you will need to think outside the box, act outside the box, and live outside the box. To do that, you must know the size and dimensions of your current box. Awareness gives you control.

CHAPTER 4:
RELUCTANT LEARNING

The Ultimate Invisible Barrier

"In times of change learners inherit the earth; while the
learned find themselves beautifully equipped to deal with a
world that no longer exists."

– Eric Hoffer

If you have never heard the expression, or someone referred to as a "reluctant earner," it is another way of calling someone a "know-it-all," or even more specifically someone who is satisfied with their knowledge. This subject, however, goes much deeper than simply warning you of becoming a "know-it-all" and teaching the value of an open mind. By the very nature of being human, the plague of reluctant learning has been, is, and always will be, a barrier. Nobody is exempt.

I refer to reluctant learning as "the ultimate invisible barrier" because most people have no idea that they are reluctant learners. To whom I'm referring are people who are oblivious to the third realm of knowledge, the realm of "we don't know what we don't know." It is invisible, and it is the ultimate! In my opinion, it is the most dangerous barrier, not only to your success, but to your life.

Three Realms of Knowledge

Let me slow down or even back up a bit and make sure you are with me on this because it is important. There are three different realms of knowledge.

1. The first realm contains *those things you know you know*. For example, you know that you know how to read. I know that I know how to type, speak English, walk, drive, ride a bike, count money, tell time, etc.

2. The second realm contains *those things you know you don't know*. For example, I know that I don't know how to perform open-heart surgery, speak Cantonese, juggle four tennis balls, navigate a double-black diamond run, etc. I know I don't know those things.

Before I address the third realm of knowledge, I want to mention that we, as humans, go through our entire lives making decisions based on the knowledge within the first two realms; what we know we know and what we know we don't know. When making decisions, big and small, we tend to give heed to the knowledge we already have but will completely ignore the knowledge and information we do not have; or even more damning, the knowledge and information we don't know we don't have. That is the third realm.

3. The third realm contains *those things we don't know we don't know*. It is in the third realm where all the difference is made. It is here where breakthroughs and triumphs are experienced. It is in this realm where you get from where you are to where you want to go. The knowledge you currently possess has gotten you to where you are today, and that knowledge will keep you exactly where you are until you begin to access the third realm.

A perfect example is that if I asked any random person for a sure-fire way to lose weight, 99% of the time I would get an answer along the lines of "eat less and exercise more." This is not groundbreaking information, yet America is more obese than it has ever been. In fact, I heard on the radio recently that in the United States, due to obesity and the complications that accompany it, the babies being born today will be the first generation ever expected to live fewer years than their parents. As a people, we know how to lose weight, yet we don't do it. There is something about losing weight that we don't know that we don't know.

Another example is that if I asked a random group of people how to become wealthy, the answer would be something along the lines of "spend less than you earn and invest the difference." Again, nothing groundbreaking here either, yet according to the U.S. Department of Health and Human Services, 94% of America's population will reach the retirement age of 65 either dead or dead broke. There is obviously information that 94% of the population doesn't know that they don't know about becoming wealthy. The fact that "lose weight" and "make more money" are the two most popular New Year's resolutions year in and year out is proof there is an invisible barrier around these two subjects.

> Education is what remains after one has forgotten everything he learned in school.
>
> – *Albert Einstein*

The above examples are two very general ones, so here's a specific example that I experience on a regular basis. Being that my primary business is showing people how to get on the fast track to creating wealth and experiencing the good life through real estate investing, I frequently find myself discussing real estate investing with a wide variety of people. Surprisingly, a group of people who have a huge invisible barrier about this particular subject are real estate agents. It is amazing how this group believes in, promotes, and facilitates the practice of real estate investing, yet the vast majority do not invest themselves. In fact, I meet a surprising number of real estate agents who don't own any real estate, including their primary residence. Even more surprising is how reluctant they are to entertain the most simple advice or possible solutions to their inability to practice what they preach. There is obviously something that those who do not invest don't know that they don't know, or else they would, yes?

The real estate agent example illustrates how easy it can be to slip into the delusion of being well versed, adept, or an expert at something, and shutting off additional information that would make a difference. The real danger to considering yourself an expert or one who is "in the know" is that you limit what's possible for yourself, your relationships, and your business.

> It's what you learn after you know it all that counts.
>
> – Harry S. Truman

In the eyes of a student there are millions of options, while in the eyes of an expert there are but a few. The lesson here is to always be a student. Never consider yourself an expert.

Thomas Szasz, Professor Emeritus of Psychiatry at the State University of New York Health and Science Center in Syracuse, New York, says, "Every act of conscious learning requires the willingness to suffer an injury to one's self-esteem. That is why young children, before they are aware of their own self-importance, learn so easily."

If you made the decision one day to take up tennis, and someone handed you a racket and then proceeded to teach you how to hit a backhand, as a new student the instructor would have your undivided attention. You would be open. You would be willing. You would be open and willing with enthusiasm. The beginner has hundreds, even thousands, of options open to them. The beginner will try anything and everything to execute a good backhand, but if you talk to an expert tennis player, they know only one way. This is not only true for tennis, but for your relationships, your business, your finances, your health – everything. You can be so clogged up with what you know that there isn't room for anything new, particularly something that could enhance and improve your performance and results. Be wary of experts, particularly if you are one yourself.

> Some people will never learn anything, for this reason, because they understand everything too soon.
>
> – Alexander Pope

In 2004, when he was at the top of his game, miles ahead of his competition, Tiger Woods completely overhauled his golf swing for the second time in his professional career, improving both times.

Take two lessons from Tiger:

1. There is always room for improvement.
2. Be a student, always. Your greatness depends on it.

CHAPTER 5:
THE NINE PERSONALITY TRAITS OF SUCCESSFUL PEOPLE

"Not to be cheered by praise, not to be grieved by blame,
but to know thoroughly one's own virtues or powers are the
characteristics of an excellent man."

– Satchel Paige

Thus far we have focused primarily on what may have been present in the past that stifled or thwarted your success. In this chapter we will explore what might have been missing that the presence of which would have made a difference in your success.

There are several commonalities among successful people, specifically their personality traits or "ways of being." My experience and observations have allowed me to narrow them down to these nine: Integrity, Honesty, Responsibility, Belief, Confidence, Charity, Courage, Communication, and Goal Orientation.

1. Integrity

As I have been able to observe these nine commonalities among successful people, I have been unable to determine an order of importance of these traits. One, however, does seem to stand out, and that character trait is integrity. It creates an environment of functionality and workability directly impacting every area of life; and with an environment where things function and work, performance is enhanced, producing favorable results.

J.C. Penney – businessman, entrepreneur, and co-founder of the department store J.C. Penney Company – became one of the richest men in America based on one rule: the Golden Rule. It is a rule based on reciprocity, an ethical code that states one has a right to just treatment and a responsibility to ensure justice for others. The Golden Rule has its roots in a wide range of cultures, religions and disciplines. Pittacus, a Greek philosopher, stated it as, "Do not to your neighbor what you would take ill from him." Being a person of integrity is paramount to one's success when dealing with other people, yet it needs to be first implemented when dealing with one's self.

To experience quantum leaps in your results, make it a rule to say what you are going to do, do what you say, and do it for no other reason than because you said so. If you live your life by 1) the Golden Rule, and 2) making declarations backed by follow-through, everything will miraculously, almost magically, come together and start to work. Without integrity, nothing works. Integrity is a prerequisite for workability, and workability is a prerequisite for performance, achievement, and success.

2. Honesty

A very successful businessman once told me that when it comes to producing success and wealth, there is no more important quality a human can have than that of honesty. Be impeccably honest with yourself and others because all successful relationships and businesses are based on trust. Honesty begets trust. Develop a reputation for being honest. People will give their friendship, their loyalty and their business to honest people.

3. Responsibility

Success on any major scale requires one to accept responsibility for their actions and their results. In the final evaluation, the one quality that all successful people have is the willingness to take responsibility. It takes a big person to step up and take responsibility, not only for their own actions, but for those of the people they lead. Be responsible.

How does anyone succeed at anything if they are responsible for nothing? John F. Kennedy took on the responsibility, and declared it before it was even known how it would be accomplished, of putting a man on the moon. Gandhi took on the responsibility for the liberation of an entire country. Would we even know his name if he had not? Dr. Martin Luther King, Jr. took on the responsibility for the civil rights of all human beings. Would we even know his name if he had not?

If I could sum up my regrets into one, it would be that I regret not taking more responsibility for my business the first time around. I placed so much of my destiny in the hands of others, sitting around waiting for other people to come through. BIG mistake! Take responsibility for your own efforts, mistakes, and results...and greatness will be yours.

4. Belief

As I work my way through these nine character traits, I find myself thinking for each one, "Oh yes, this is the most important one," only to realize that all nine play integral parts to one's success. Belief is no exception. Belief is paramount. The belief in one's dreams, the belief in one's self, and the belief that what one is doing will manifest their dreams could quite possibly be the one trait that without it, success will forever elude you.

Your beliefs will change everything. You are what you believe, and others will perceive you that way as well. That's how important your beliefs are. That could be interpreted as something daunting, or as an opportunity. Change your beliefs, whether intentionally or not, and you change your life.

That being the case, my advice to anybody who seeks success is to "believe BIG," and here's why: The size of your success will be determined by the size of your belief and ideas. Think small and expect small achievements. Think big and expect big achievements. You'll want to keep this at front of mind, too; big ideas and goals are often easier — certainly no more difficult — than small ideas and goals.

I've witnessed time and time again that belief in big results is the power and the driving force behind all great accomplishment, regardless of whether you're dealing with business, art, relationships, sports, or science. A strong belief system is behind every successful business, church, and political organization. Those who believe they can move mountains, do. Belief triggers the power to *do*. When you believe you *can* do it, the *how* will develop like magic. Change your beliefs, and you will change your life. Belief in success is an essential ingredient in attaining it.

5. Self-Esteem and Confidence

I waffled over the idea of including this in the description of "belief," but as it serves as a natural transition, it seemed more appropriate to distinguish it in its own category as self-esteem and confidence.

That first step is to believe in yourself and believe you can succeed.

For a few, this is seemingly a natural belief, and because it is, the few succeed. However, for most, this is a very unnatural way of living. As mentioned before, we experienced a pivotal decision early in life where we decided we weren't good enough and forever sentenced ourselves to a life of self-doubt. For most, self-esteem and confidence must be generated or earned. When you venture into thinking big and dreaming big, when you undertake the pursuit of your dream, when you dare to endure the pain, sacrifice, and friction from external sources, environments and people, you will find that you genuinely impress yourself; the end result being an authentic sense of self-esteem and confidence.

Self-esteem and confidence are extremely powerful, to the point they are the primary sources of your achievement; but even more powerful is the lack of self-esteem and confidence. On a daily basis we destroy ourselves with cynicism and delusion, as effectively as rain erodes hillsides, locusts ravage crops, and bombs destroy cities.

Self-esteem, self-acceptance, and confidence may be the ultimate definitions of success. Material possessions can be obtained with relative ease, yet the transformation of our deepest thoughts and learning to love and trust ourselves can be a monumental, and tragically an elusive, quest.

The Success Cycle

The authentic creation of confidence begins with the awareness of something called the "success cycle." A mentor of mine taught this to me. It's rather elementary, but because it is so basic, it works.

In a nutshell, confidence breeds confidence.

In detail, confidence begins with education and training, then confidence leads to activity, activity then produces results, results manifest success, success creates more confidence, and around and around you go. (See the diagram on the following page.) The most powerful distinction surrounding the success cycle is that either you're on it, or you're not. Knowing that there's no in-between makes it very easy to determine if you're on track to achievement or not.

As mentioned previously, you are what you believe, and others will perceive you that way. As a matter of fact, it goes even deeper than that. Being what you believe yourself to be in front of others acts as a self-fulfilling prophecy, meaning that you will be how you believe others perceive you to be. Awareness, and the use, of this distinction can significantly impact your performance on the success cycle. Five simple practices for your day-to-day activities that will convey to others that "I am confident, I am really confident" are:

1. Always sit in the front row.
2. Always make eye contact with people.
3. Walk 25% faster.
4. Speak up.
5. Smile big.

What you'll really want to get from this section is that self-esteem and confidence are acquired and developed. No one is born with

"it." The people you know who radiate confidence, who have
conquered worry, who are at ease everywhere they go, who are
undaunted regardless of the challenge, acquired their confidence,
every bit of it. By understanding how the success cycle works, you
can, too; and nothing – absolutely nothing – in life will give you
more comfort and delight than knowing you're on the road to
success and achievement. Later I'll show you how to monitor
whether you're on or off.

THE SUCCESS CYCLE

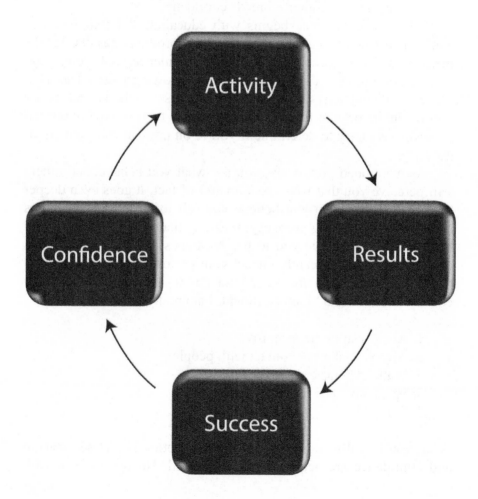

6. Charity

This section doesn't require a whole lot of explanation. Regard for other people is an innate quality of all human beings, and it doesn't exclude the successful. Names like Bill Gates, Brad Pitt, Oprah Winfrey, and Bono – the list of successful charitable people is endless – should be proof enough that giving is a common trait of the successful.

It's been said that we make a living by what we get, but we make a life by what we give. A fulfilled life is given to you by what you give to others. Einstein said, "It is every man's obligation to put back into the world at least the equivalent of what he takes out of it." The successful do.

7. Courage

Courage is not the *absence of fear*, but rather *action in the presence of fear*.

Fear can be a good thing. Fear is a great teacher. I have come to know the "fear zone" as the "money zone." If money is at the foundation of your definition of success, you'll want to know that it will never be yours until you are courageous. Living in fear, or living with a lack of courage, is the biggest success killer there is. Standing up to fear, taking its measure, refusing to let it shape and define your life is a staple among achievers. Your life will expand, or shrink, in direct proportion to the size of your courage.

Winston Churchill said it best: "Courage is going from failure to failure without losing enthusiasm." It takes courage to stick it out, to keep trying, to get up after each time you're knocked down. Success is the child of persistence, audacity and courage. Persistence and audacity is ongoing sacrifice, without a guarantee or even the likelihood of a reward. Wherever you see a successful business, a successful organization, or a successful person, you will know a series of persistent and courageous decisions and actions preceded that success.

Success comes about as a result of habit. We *become* courageous by *doing* courageous acts. Like confidence, you gain courage by every experience in which you really stop to look fear in the face. Courage comes about by consistently doing the things you think you cannot do.

Courage is so important to your success because, with courage, you will dare to take risks, brush off adversity, muster the strength for empathy and acquire the wisdom of, and discretion for, humility.

Without courage, there is no integrity. When the Cowardly Lion boldly pulled back the curtain to reveal the Wizard of Oz, he was surprised to find a frail old man at the controls. The more I face my fears, like the Cowardly Lion did, the more I realize the great truth that there is nothing to fear except fear itself. Whatever worthwhile endeavor you choose to take on, you will need courage. Regardless of the course you choose, the road you travel, or the dreams you pursue, there will always be someone there to tell you that it can't be done. Circumstances and evidence will frequently appear to support the opinions of your critics. To envision a dream, declare its possibility, create a plan of action, and follow it through to the end requires courage equivalent to that generated by a fireman rushing a burning building, a U.S. Marine advancing towards enemy lines, or a David slaying Goliath. To pursue your dreams and proceed contrary to the predominant opinions of your family, friends, associates, and the people you interact with on a daily basis, is perhaps the most profound act of courage you can perform.

8. Mutual Understanding and Good Communication

Habit #5 from the classic by Stephen Covey, _The 7 Habits of Highly Effective People_, is _Seek First to Understand, Then to be Understood_. Everything you will ever want out of life that ultimately defines your success will be accessed or acquired through the cooperation of other people. Great communication is required to elicit the cooperation of people, and it is a common trait found in successful people. You will undoubtedly find as many communication styles as you will successful people, but the common denominator is that they are effective.

Your success will be in direct proportion to your ability to connect with people, and people predominantly use language to connect. The most basic and powerful way to connect to another person is to listen. Just listen.

God gave us two ears and one mouth, and some of the best advice I've ever been given is to use them proportionately. Listen twice as much as you speak.

The most important thing we can give to another person is our attention. I have found to evoke another's interest in you, you must first be interested in them. An authentic silence with genuine interest in another often has far more power to connect than the most well-intentioned words. When someone is talking to you, listen completely. Most people never listen.

Many attempts to communicate are nullified by saying too much. The problem with saying too much is that it can create the illusion that communication has been accomplished.

There are three sources of hindrance that will derail your train to success, and they are:

1. Foiled or thwarted intention
2. Unfulfilled expectations
3. Undelivered communication

Two-thirds (sources two and three, above) of what will halt your journey, stifle your results, and produce disappointment can be virtually eliminated with direct and effective communication.

9. Goal-Oriented

If you don't know where you are going, any road will get you there. The logic is inarguable. It is vital to any endeavor's fulfillment to begin with the end in mind. Establishing the desired outcome before taking the first step will eliminate counterproductive confusion and frustration.

Ralph Waldo Emerson once said, "The world makes way for the man who knows where he is going." James Cash Penney, co-founder of the J.C. Penney Company, said, "Give me a stock clerk with a goal and I'll give you a man who will make history. Give me a man with no goals and I'll give you a stock clerk." I don't know about you, but the profound words of Emerson and J.C. Penney are enough reason for me to always have goals and keep them updated. Goals are not only absolutely necessary to motivate us and keep us on track, but they are essential to keeping us alive.

"Try not to become a man of success, but rather try to become a man of value," are the words of Albert Einstein. The more accomplishments I chalk up, I have found that it is who you become along the way in the pursuit of your goals that is the true reward. The journey to success and the experience you will acquire while performing what is necessary to achieve your goals are what creates a person of value.

CHAPTER 6:
THE POWER OF
QUESTIONS

An Unknown Step

"Quality questions create a quality life. Successful people
ask better questions, and as a result, they get better
answers."

– Tony Robbins

One practice that is as responsible for my success as any other is the
use of questions. The use of properly asked questions is one of your
most valuable tools in getting where you want to go, and that has to
do with whether you are asking questions of someone else or asking
questions of yourself.

I have come to know, and trust, that my brain (and yours) will
remarkably answer any question asked of it. Here's a great example
that I use all the time, with others and myself. Any time the response
to a question is, "I don't know," I immediately follow the response
with "If you did know, what would the answer be?" This is not
groundbreaking, I know. Many of you reading this have heard this
question asked, and likely multiple times from various people in
various environments. It often times is received as a flippant,
sarcastic, or jesting response.

If you ignore the irreverent and cheeky tone that often
accompanies the question, you will notice it almost always evokes
an answer where there wasn't one before. I don't understand how
this mocking question, "If you did know, what would your answer

be?" stimulates the brain to answer, but it does almost every single time. What the question demonstrates is that the brain will provide an answer with relative ease in the face of no answer. For those very rare times it doesn't provide an answer, the next question is "How or where could you find out?" The pitfall most people fall into is that they fail to ask another question after the response "I don't know."

Tony Robbins references the human brain as the most powerful computer in the world and that it can answer any question asked of it. Of all the personal development information I've injected into my mind, this one concept mentioned by Robbins quite possibly has had the greatest impact on my success. From that concept I have developed two rules that I live by with regard to questions.

Rule #1:
Ask yourself the right questions—empowering questions.

Rule #2:
Answer the questions honestly and authentically.

What do I mean by empowering questions? Based on the commonality that most people do not ask themselves empowering questions, perhaps it's easier to illustrate the answer by giving you some examples of disempowering questions.

"Why does this always happen to me?"
"Why can't I ever get a break?"
"Why don't I ever win?"
"Why does the other guy always get the promotion?"

These are examples of *disempowering* questions. Do any of them sound familiar? These types of questions elicit a negative answer that will undoubtedly inspire negative thinking, and we know where that leads.

In situations where you may ask yourself (and this is one question that always plagued me) "Why does this always happen to me?" you will want to replace that question with something like,

"How can I minimize the possibility of this happening again?" or "Where is the opportunity in this situation?" You will find, with a little bit of attention and intention, that answers to what afflicts you will come to the forefront of your thinking easier and more quickly than you thought possible. Once your brain has revealed an answer or two (and there will be multiple answers if you keep asking), the key is to focus on the answers and then act.

A cherished mentor of mine once told me during a moment of misfortune and calamity (and I mentioned this before), "Matt, stop focusing on what is happening…focus on what you want to have happen." A well-thought-out empowering question will redirect your focus to what you want to have happen and pull you through adversity.

Rule #2 says that you ask empowering questions and answer them honestly and authentically. Some of my biggest results have been produced by getting real with myself, answering my questions honestly and completely. For example, when experiencing a lull in my direct sales business I asked myself, "Am I doing everything I know to do?" "Am I doing what I know to do to the best of my ability?" These are two questions that can serve you in many different areas of your life, but only if you're honest with your answer. I find that in most situations we all know exactly what to do; where we fall short is *doing* what we know. Do yourself a favor and check in with yourself every once in a while with those two questions.

Old habits can be tough to break. When first setting out to implement the practice of asking yourself empowering questions, it can be difficult to 1) stop yourself before asking a disempowering question, and 2) formulating consistently effective empowering questions.

Knowing that from experience, I have assembled a list of twenty-five empowering questions that I have found useful in getting me out of potentially sticky situations, furthering my personal development, and staying on track toward my goals. Until you get the hang of formulating the most effective and empowering questions for yourself, feel free to use, modify and share some of mine.

25 Empowering Questions

1. If money weren't an object, would this be a good business decision?
2. If money weren't an object, would this decision be in alignment with my dreams and/or morals?
3. What can I do right now that would move me one step closer to my goal(s)?
4. How can I minimize the impact of this problem?
5. How can I minimize the possibility of this problem reoccurring?
6. Am I enviable? If not, why not? How can I make myself more enviable?
7. What's the next step?
8. Who do I know that could help me with this?
9. Is there anyone that I can delegate this to?
10. Is this the best use of my time, or should I hire someone else to do it? (Visit www.Elance.com)
11. What can I do that would make me even more effective?
12. What can I learn from this?
13. How can I turn this problem around, and enjoy the process?
14. Where is the opportunity in this situation?
15. If I were mentoring someone in my situation, what would I tell them?
16. What is one way I could change how I conduct my business that would cause me to enjoy it even more?
17. What about my current situation can I laugh at?
18. What do I have right now that I'm grateful for?
19. What am I excited about right now? Or, what could I be excited about right now?
20. What am I proud of right now? Or, what could I be proud of right now?
21. For my life to be perfect, what would I have to change?
22. If I could drop everything right now, what would I go do? And whom would I do it with?

    a. What type of income would I have to be earning on a monthly basis to have the type of freedom to do that right now?

    b. How long will it take, doing what I'm currently doing, to earn that type of income? Am I content with that answer, or should I start looking for something else to do?

23. What is one risk I can take today that will move me closer to my goals?

24. What are three things I do on a regular basis that hinder the pursuit of my goals?

25. Are my dreams big enough, or have they waned with age?

CHAPTER 7:
CREATING A
COMPELLING FUTURE

It's no coincidence the last example of an empowering question in the previous chapter was, "Are my dreams big enough, or have they waned with age?"

When you were five years old, what did you want to be when you grew up? What did you want to do? What did you want to have?

What were the answers to those three questions when you were ten years old? Fifteen years old? Twenty years old?

What are the answers to those questions right now? Are you who you originally dreamed of being? Are you doing what you originally dreamed of doing? Do you have everything you originally dreamed of having? Or did you settle? Did you once dream of being a rock star? A ballerina? An astronaut? An actress? Where did "reality" kick in and redirect you? At what age did you dream of doing what you're currently doing? Did you ever? Have you settled?

> If you dream it, and you believe it, it's not a dream. It's reality waiting to happen.
>
> – *Matt Theriault*

Certainly, our interests will change with age. So it's not necessarily sticking with the same dream throughout life to which I'm referring, but it is the size of the dream. As you moved your way through life, your childhood passion of exploring outer space might have morphed into a passion of discovering a cure for cancer, eradicating world hunger, or inventing the next "thing" that makes the world an easier place to live. The question is, "Are you pursuing your passion, your dream?"

Dreams and passions can, and often do, change. What you will want to monitor for change, however, is the size of your dreams and passions. Throughout the years have they increased or decreased in size?

If you dream it, and you believe it, it's not a dream. It's reality waiting to happen. The world is replete with evidence that this is so. Bruce Springsteen once dreamed of being a rock star. Tiger Woods once dreamed of being the world's greatest golfer. Robert DeNiro once dreamed of being an actor. Neil Armstrong once dreamed of going to the Moon. Benjamin Franklin once dreamed of harnessing electricity. Mahatma Gandhi once dreamed of a free India. Martin Luther King, Jr. once dreamed of raising the consciousness of civil rights and ending racial segregation.

They all had a dream, they all believed in their dream, they all pursued their dream and they all achieved their dream. What would our world look like if they hadn't?

I attended a seminar in which Dr. Jay Grossman, a dentist, stood up to share an experience he had while running his non-profit organization, Homeless Not Toothless (http://www.HomelessNotToothless.org). His organization has been able to establish a program for homeless people in Los Angeles to get free dental care. I believe his program has expanded nationally since. At this seminar Jay shared an encounter he had with one homeless patient during his free examination. The patient was blessed with the good fortune to have met in his lifetime both Mahatma Gandhi and Martin Luther King, Jr. The homeless man went on to share his experience with the dentist, and the two parts of the story that stood out for me the most was first, that he had the nerve to ask both Gandhi and King, "If you were to live your life over, what would you have done differently?" The second part that stood out was that both Gandhi and King had had the exact same answer to that question, "I wish I would've dreamed bigger."

When I heard the story, the hairs on my arms stood on end. In fact, I still get the chills when I tell the story today. It's a great story and I have no way of verifying its authenticity, but knowing what

Gandhi and King dreamed, believed and achieved in their lives, it's not difficult to accept the story as unequivocal truth.

What I want you to get out of this is that no dream is too big. There is magic in dreaming and thinking big. One of my favorite books is _The Magic of Thinking Big_ by David J. Schwartz, Ph.D. When this book was first recommended to me, my initial thought was, "Not another book on positive thinking!" However, I trusted the referral source, and I was pleasantly surprised. The book is replete with "meat." Get it.

The great artist Michelangelo once said, "The greatest danger for most of us is not that our aim is too high and we miss it, but that it is too low and we reach it."

Many are waiting for Mahatma Gandhi and Martin Luther King to come back – but they are gone. We are it. It is up to us. It is up to you. Dream BIG, and believe.

Don't be afraid to take risks. Risks can be a telling gauge of people. People who avoid them do so to protect what they have. People who take them frequently end up with having more. What I've come to know is that if you risk nothing, you risk everything.

For a dream to come true, you must first have one. Allow yourself to dream really big. Big dreams lend themselves to big thoughts. Big thoughts create big emotions and foster passion. Not only does a dream give you something to aim for, but when a burning desire to achieve that dream is in place, the dream calls you into action. When you discover your passion, your mission, your purpose, you will

> What inevitably holds most people back isn't the quality of, or size of, their dream, but the lack of faith they have in themselves.
>
> – Matt Theriault

feel its demand. Big emotions and passion will lead to big conversations and actions. Your dream will fill you with enthusiasm and excitement to get to work. It will burn.

When the vision is crystal clear and the burn is in place, the daily decisions to take action become easy. Those actions will eventually become habits that support the pursuit of your dream. Your habits will shape your character to that of a person capable of achieving your dream, creating a compelling future for you to live into, and the future we create for ourselves gives us who we are today. But, before anything else, you must have a dream. It all begins with the dream.

What inevitably holds most people back isn't the quality of, or size of, their dream, but the lack of faith they have in themselves. Your biggest obstacle on the road to realizing your dreams is the belief that the dream is beyond reach, or more specifically, beyond your reach. This belief stems from the many suppressive forces we encounter that cause us to settle for mediocrity.

Whatever dream you're pursuing, people will always – and I mean always – tell you, "You can't do this," or "You'll never be able to do that." These naysayers are inescapable. But you can do it. There will always be critics trying to steal your dreams. Don't let them in. The world belongs to people who say, "I can." It will seem impossible until it's done. The importance of dreaming big cannot be underestimated. The size of your dream is the first line of defense against negative people, environment, and most of all, negative thoughts. It's paramount that you revisit your dream constantly. Maintain a clear vision of that dream. It is not uncommon for me to review my dreams (I have them displayed in a "dream book") two to three times a day. Surround yourself with literature, sounds, images and people that remind you, and support your pursuit, of your dream.

Don't let the details block your view.

Don't let doubt and indecision hinder your performance.

Life is short.

Aim high, move fast and focus.

And above all:

Dream.

Believe.

Achieve.

The Placebo Effect

Allow me to expand on the power of belief for a minute and bring to your consciousness a phenomenon known as the placebo effect. It's that important.

When an inactive and powerless substance improves the health of, or cures, an ill patient, the effect is called the placebo effect. Although the actual mechanism that produces the results of a placebo is still a scientific mystery, enough research has been conducted to strongly suggest that it's the patient's expectation, or "belief," that cures whatever ails them. The expectancy effect can be enhanced

> What you believe in most comes about.
>
> – *Matt Theriault*

through factors such as the enthusiasm of the doctor, differences in size and color of placebo pills, or the use of other inventions such as injections. In one study, the response to a placebo pill increased from 44% to 62% when the doctor gave it with "warmth, attention, and confidence."

For most of my life I underestimated the power of belief. It was not until I witnessed the placebo effect firsthand that I understood the true power of belief. My understanding of the placebo effect can be summed up as "expectations supported with confidence." Expectations supported with confidence equates to belief. Beliefs are a prevailing character trait among the successful. The Napoleon Hill quote, "What the mind can conceive and believe, it can achieve," is the foundation of Hill's philosophy and bolsters the foundation of every successful person's character.

Here's why: placebos work.

What you believe in most comes about. You are then what you believe others believe you to be. And you are to them, in large part, what you believe yourself to be. Your belief in yourself will inspire it in others. General Colin Powell refers to belief as a "force multiplier." If your belief in yourself is lacking, transform your image to that which you want to become. Football star Dionne Sanders used to say something to the effect of "If you look good, you feel good. If you feel good, you play good. If you play good, you win." Like it or not, your image and appearance are a great place to start when your belief in yourself is low. If you truly believe in yourself, others will too.

The force and power of belief have been ingrained in American culture since the early twentieth century via the children's story, _The Little Engine That Could_. "I think I can, I think I can..." could be the greatest belief you could adopt on the road to success.

A belief that has served me well for years, and has pulled me through my lowest points in life, is, "This too shall pass, and the best is yet to come." Regardless of what you're experiencing in life, whether bad or good, knowing and believing it is only temporary will foster persistence and keep you grounded.

Aim high, move fast, and focus. Dream. Believe. Achieve.

Which Dream to Follow?

A razor-sharp focus is important to achieving your dreams, but where to direct that focus?

There is a shortcut to figuring this out. Ask yourself, "What am I passionate about?"

When your heart rate increases a bit while thinking of your dream, that's the one to pursue.

When you find yourself excited to talk about it, that's the one to pursue.

If you find yourself feeling lukewarm about an idea, ditch it.

If you're finding it challenging to come up with a passionate and unique idea, it's okay. Look around you. Who is doing something that you respect and admire? There's nothing wrong with eying someone else's dream and morphing it into your own. Inspiration comes from everywhere. Inspiration can come from within your own industry or a competitor. Much of this book is inspired by other great writers and thinkers who came before me. It evolved from myriad concepts, faiths, disciplines, techniques, strategies, and systems. I haven't reinvented the wheel, merely reshaped it a bit and presented it in a different way that works for me, and in a way that can make the difference for you.

Have you ever noticed how you can hear something over and over and over again, but then one day you hear it in a different way from a different source in a different environment and it finally clicks? Your dream may come about in the same way, and if it does, it's perfectly okay.

In defining your dream, be sure to aim beyond what you are capable of. You must develop a complete disregard for where you think your abilities end. Try to do the things that you're incapable of. If you think you're unable to work for the best company in its sphere, make that your aim. If you think you're incapable of running a company, make that your aim. If you think you're unable to be on the cover of *Time* Magazine, make it your business to be there. Nothing is impossible.

Once you've decided on the dream to pursue, document it. If you don't, it's easy to lose sight. It's easy for your razor sharp focus to blur. In its simplest form, write it down. I recommend creating a dream book or vision board. For an example of a vision board and instructions on how to create your own, visit http://theDoOverGuy.com/YourVision. Create as much detail as possible around the dream. Use emotional images and bright colors. You will need to call on these images frequently to maintain your focus, to get you past the obstacles, to pass the tests.

Clarity around your dream cannot be underestimated. The ability to clearly articulate your dream to others is paramount, and I will expound on this in a later chapter. To attain your dream you will need the cooperation of people. People will follow someone with a clear vision. People love to be around and help people with a clear vision. Why? In many cases, people are unclear about their own dream and they will follow and support someone with purpose, confidence and clarity.

CHAPTER 8:
COMMITMENTS AND PRIORITIES

"The quality of a person's life is in direct proportion to their commitment to excellence, regardless of their chosen field of endeavor."

– Vince Lombardi

Commitment is a funny thing in the sense that I don't have to tell you to be committed because you are already committed to something. What is that? It's simple. Everything you have in your life right now is what you're committed to. If there are things that are missing in your life, it's because you haven't made a commitment to them. If you don't have as much money as you'd like, it's because you haven't committed to getting it. If you don't have good relationships at work, it's because you haven't made a commitment to creating them. If you don't have a peaceful life, it's because you haven't made a commitment to it.

Unless a commitment is made, there are only false promises and empty hopes. I know each and every human, including you, is committed, but to what? The answer, actually, is very easy, possibly painful, but easy. Are you ready for this? Regardless of what you declare your dreams to be, you are committed to exactly what you have in your life right now – nothing more, nothing less. You can't be committed to anything else, and here's what I mean.

Imagine a thermostat in an office building is set to 72°. When the temperature drops below 72°, the thermostat recognizes "danger, it's too cold" and the heater turns on, increasing the temperature back to 72°. When the temperature rises above 72°, the A/C recognizes "danger, it's too hot" and it begins to operate, bringing the temperature back down to 72°. The thermostat is committed to 72°.

What does this have to do with your commitment? Each and every human being has an internal "comfort" thermostat, or what I call your "survival" thermostat. When the going gets tough, the heater kicks in. When the going gets good, the A/C kicks in.

I share this with you to illustrate that you have an autopilot working to ensure your survival. It's your internal auto-commitment.

Although this automated mechanism keeps you alive, it also *prevents* you from achieving your dreams and desires.

When I say you are committed to everything you have in your life right now, and if you are not satisfied with what you have, it is a result of your internal auto-commitment. Your auto-commitment has provided you everything it was programmed to provide, and that includes your relationships, your appearance, your assets, your liabilities and your bank account. To be committed to something other than what your survival thermostat is committed to, you must choose to be.

If it is success you want, regardless of what area of your life you want it in, it is success you must commit to. Commitment is a choice, and unless you consciously make this choice, your auto-commitment will maintain a comfortable 72° the rest of your life. Actually, let me correct that...it's not that easy. Your auto-commitment will struggle to maintain a comfortable 72°, but it will operate most often between 68° and 71° while the heater fluctuates in intensity, resulting in struggle and frustration. Because of your auto-commitment, you have a probable and almost certain future. Don't believe me? Looking back at your life, do you recognize patterns? Do you see common traits in your past relationships? Do you see patterns in the fluctuation of your health or weight? Do you recognize patterns in the ebb and flow of your accomplishments and bank balance? Humans are committed to survival. How do I know? I know because you are here. You are reading this book. You are surviving. You will do whatever it takes to eat, breathe, and sleep, but anything beyond that is a conscious choice.

Most people have an interest in success, but few commit to it. There's a significant difference between interest and commitment. Understanding the difference creates clarity around what you're up to in life and allows you to be real with yourself. When you're interested in doing something, you do it only when circumstances permit. When you're committed to something, you accept no excuses, only results.

Basketball superstar Jerry West once said, "You can't get much done in life if you only work on the days when you feel good." It takes commitment to work on the days you don't feel good. For example, you are committed to breathing. That's a commitment. Imagine yourself swimming in the ocean. You take a deep breath and dive below. Once your lungs run out of air, you are committed to resurfacing for a breath of oxygen – there are no excuses. You wouldn't say to yourself, "I don't really feel like getting some oxygen right now, I think I'll hang out for a while until I feel better and play with the fish in the meantime." You would never think that. There are no excuses accepted. Only the result of "oxygen" is accepted because your life depends on it.

Are you committed to your dreams and goals as if your life depends on them? If you were, they wouldn't be dreams, they would be reality. It's one thing to declare, "I'm going to be a millionaire," it's another thing entirely to declare, "Every day I will do whatever it takes to get there." One has to make that declaration every day until they arrive.

> **Most people promise according to their hopes and perform according to their fears.**
>
> *– Matt Theriault*

The achievement of your dreams and goals is assured the instant you commit yourself to it. Commitment will provide you with many things. It will inspire new realms of creativity, vision, and performance to turn our dreams into reality; and in the face of conflict and adversity, commitment produces character. The quality of your life will be in direct proportion to your commitment to your dreams. When your commitment, work, and pleasure become one, and hopefully that's beginning to appear for you by now, nothing will be impossible. Your life begins with your dreams, and life exists through your commitment.

CHAPTER 9:
PLAN THE WORK

"Our goals can only be reached through a vehicle of a plan,
in which we must fervently believe, and upon which we
must vigorously act. There is no other route to success."

– Pablo Picasso

Without a vision, a plan is worthless. If your vision isn't clear, re-read Chapter 7 before continuing. To accomplish great things, we must first dream in high-definition and believe with unwavering faith, and only then does it make sense to plan. An effective plan should begin with the end in mind – a goal. A goal must not only be aligned with your dreams, but your values.

On the road to my second success, congruency has been a powerful distinction for me. In the past, if I had set a goal that was out of accordance with my values, morals, beliefs, and dreams, I discovered it was difficult to achieve. This doesn't just apply to the goal, but the methods in achieving the goal as well. For example, if your goal is in alignment with your values, but you pursue a shortcut to your goal that is out of alignment with your values, the road to achieving that goal is riddled with bumps, potholes, booby-traps and setbacks. By taking incongruent short cuts, you will eventually recognize, often times too late, that you have injected unnecessary struggle into the pursuit of your goals.

Focused energy is much more powerful and efficient than energy dispersed. If you were to walk outside on a typical fall day and feel the sun against your face, it would feel pleasantly warm. Sunlight is an example of energy dispersed. Conversely, that same sunlight directed toward a dry autumn leaf passing through a magnifying glass would burn a hole in it. That is energy *focused*.

That sunlight focused with enough intensity can produce a laser that cuts through steel. Your mental focus works in precisely the same way. Focused energy is a powerful force.

Many authorities on goal-setting suggest that to maintain balance you should set goals in all areas of your life: Personal Development, Career/Business/Economic, Toys/Adventure, and Contribution. I'm going to suggest going against the grain on this. I'm going to suggest you choose one to three areas of your life that aren't working, or not working as well as you'd like them to be working, and go to work only there.

> In creating a plan, congruency is #1. Focus is #2.
>
> – *Matt Theriault*

The reason being, I've always had written goals and what I've found is this:

The more goals I have, the less I achieve.

My philosophy on why this is so has everything to do with how dispersed energy and focused energy work. I don't see anything wrong or detrimental to you having many goals, but what I'm suggesting is to focus on no more than three at a time. My rule of thumb is to focus on one to three goals for maximum effectiveness, and I will typically achieve one to three of those goals.

Focus on four to eight goals and I achieve one, maybe.

Focus on nine or more and achieve nothing.

Just as the law of diminishing returns can impact economics, it can impact your goal achievement as well. A confused, overwhelmed and unfocused mind does, and achieves, absolutely nothing. So, let's get focused.

Step 1: Defining Your Dreams and Creating Your Goals

The exercise I'm about to share with you is one that I perform twice a year. It's a brainstorming exercise that confirms that my dreams and goals are still important to me. As I shared before, it's okay to change your dreams and goals, but maintain their size: BIG.

You will want to begin with a blank piece of paper and a timer. Set the timer for ten minutes. Begin writing down your dreams and goals in these four areas of life:

1. Personal Development
2. Career/Business/Economic
3. Toys/Adventure
4. Contribution

You will want to write any and everything you can think of, big and small, short-term and long-term. Write down who you want to be, what you want to do and what you want to have. Perhaps you want to be your company's number one salesperson, the head of your own non-profit organization, a world traveler, or a lion tamer? Remember the sky's the limit and no dream is out of reach. Perhaps you want to learn a foreign language, visit every major league ballpark in the U.S., or climb Mount Kilimanjaro? It's your dream, and you get to choose what you want to do. Perhaps you want a ten-car garage filled with exotic sports cars, a ranch in Colorado, or the freedom to never have to work for somebody else again? What's important in this exercise is to keep writing for the full ten minutes. Do not let your pen leave the paper. Whatever comes to your mind, write it down. Maybe it's something as simple as acquiring the newest pair of Nike basketball shoes, or something as big as eradicating heart disease or starting the next Microsoft. This is your time to dream!

Step 2: Give Each Goal a Deadline

A dream without a deadline is just a casual notion. Go over the list you created in Step 1 and assign a simple deadline for each goal. If you would like to achieve the goal in one year, write the number one next to it; five years, the number five. Do it.

Step 3: Narrow Your Focus

From your list, circle the three single most important goals that, if you were to accomplish them this year, you would consider it your greatest year ever. Using the power of questions will help you confirm you are choosing your three most important goals. Ask yourself these questions for each one-year goal you have created. Why is this goal compelling to me? What will I gain by achieving it? What would I miss out on if I don't? Who will I be able to help because of this goal's achievement? How will that make them feel? How will that make me feel? If your answers to these questions don't stir up some burning emotions, go back to Step 1 and repeat the exercise until you can feel the burn. Do it.

Step 4: Live in the Now

See your dreams, and speak of them, as if they have already happened. In the movie *The Secret,* Bob Proctor discussed the importance of envisioning your goals as if they have already been accomplished. I'm not entirely certain as to why or how this phenomenon works, but I have noticed that it gives me a certain amount of power and definiteness of purpose around my dreams and goals. To increase your faith and confidence that your dreams and goals will be realized, I recommend you rewrite your top three goals using the sentence structure Bob Proctor shared in the movie. Using three separate pieces of paper, at the top write your goals in this format: I'm so happy and grateful now that... (my goal) *I am earning ten thousand dollars a month in passive income.*

Of course you will insert your own goal, and you can modify the sentence however you'd like, but you will want to maintain two elements for this to be effective.

1. Write your goal in the present tense, and
2. Be as specific as possible. Do it.

Step 5: Begin with the Destination in Mind

In the pursuit of a goal, this is a vital step that is often underestimated or ignored. You must know where you are going in order to get there. If you do not, any road will get you there. So, begin with the destination in mind. You already have your three goals written at the top of three separate pieces of paper. At the bottom of each page, re-write the goal and give it a deadline. You should now have three pages, each having present tense sentences at the top and bottom with a deadline.

I am so happy and greatful now that I am earning $10,000 a month in passive income.

$10,000 a month in passive income by July 1st.

Step 6: Reverse Engineer: Milestones and Minorstones

Rather than starting from your current place and determining the path you will take to achieve your goal, we will start at the end and reverse engineer the path all the way back to where you are today. We will do this using what I call "Milestones." We will create Major Milestones and Minor Milestones, establishing the Major Milestones first. Using the example illustrated on this page, the goal is to create $10,000 a month in passive income through real estate investments. Beginning there and working back, a milestone that would have to be reached just prior to its achievement would be $8,000 a month in passive income. Just prior to that would be $6,000 a month, then $4,000, then $2,000, then $1,000 a month in passive income.

I am so happy and greatful now that I am earning $10,000 a month in passive income.

M $1,000 per month in passive income.

M $2,000 per month in passive income.

M $4,000 per month in passive income.

M $6,000 per month in passive income.

M $8,000 per month in passive income.

$10,000 a month in passive income by July 1st.

Once you have established your Major Milestones, you will want to remove your focus from the end goal and now place your focus entirely on your first Major Milestone. You will now reverse engineer again from that Major Milestone and create five Minor Milestones ("Minorstones"). What has to be accomplished just prior to achieving $1,000 of passive income might be "the closing of escrow." Just prior to that might be "the opening of escrow." Prior to that might be "the submission of an offer to purchase." Prior to that might be "the locating of a property that pays $1,000 in passive income." Prior to that might be "the establishment of the markets in which I want to invest."

Reverse engineer each of your three goals in the same manner. The roadmap to your dreams is almost magically appearing. As you achieve each Major Milestone you will then create five new Minorstones in the same way you did the first five, by reverse engineering. Lessons will undoubtedly be learned along the way, revealing information you didn't know that you didn't know when your roadmap was first created. It's been said that the Apollo 11 mission on its way to the Moon was off course 97% of the time, continually making minor adjustments placing it back on course. You will likely experience a similar statistic on your way to your goals. Don't get frustrated when you seemingly get knocked off course, just adjust. If this strategy put a man on the Moon, it will work for your goals, too. Do it.

I am so happy and greatful now that I am earning $10,000 a month in passive income.

☐ Establish which market to invest in.

☐ Locate $1,000 income generating property.

☐ Submit Offer to Purchase

☐ Open escrow

☐ Close escrow!

☑ $1,000 per month in passive income.

☑ $2,000 per month in passive income.

☑ $4,000 per month in passive income.

☑ $6,000 per month in passive income.

☑ $8,000 per month in passive income.

$10,000 a month in passive income by July 1st.

Step 7: Small Daily Tasks

I am a big believer in setting small easy tasks. I believe in small easy tasks because they generate multiple experiences of easy success. It keeps you on the "success cycle." There is nothing more motivating on the path to the achievement of your most important goals than knowing you are progressively moving closer to them every day. In a nutshell, success breeds success (*à la* the *Success Cycle*).

When a mentor of mine introduced me to the success cycle, he said, "Either you're on the success cycle, or you're not."

As a refresher, the success cycle works like this:

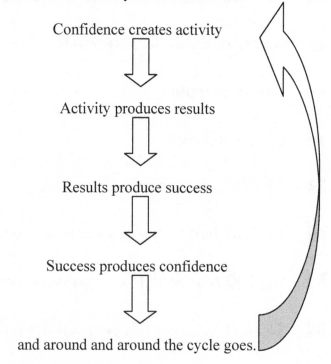

Confidence creates activity

Activity produces results

Results produce success

Success produces confidence

and around and around the cycle goes.

Either you're on it, or you're not.

You will create these small and easy daily tasks via a daily to-do list. As we were focused on the first Major Milestone to create our five Minorstones, we will now place our focus solely on the first Minorstone to create our daily to-do list. To stay consistent with our previous example, that milestone is "the establishment of the markets in which I want to invest." Small and easy daily activities focused on this Minorstone might consist of:

1. Conduct a "Google Search" for top ten cashflowing real estate markets.
2. Call my mentor to get his opinion.
3. Make a list of three investors with cashflowing real estate and call them for their opinions.
4. Conduct preliminary searches based off the opinions I collected to confirm if it's the right market for me.

You can see how these four activities for the day are small and easy. The achievement of the first Minorstone could very well be achieved on the very first day on the road to your goals. How would that make you feel to knock down the first Minorstone on the first or second day? Would you not be inspired to tackle the next Minorstone ASAP? To achieve anything you set your mind on, you will create one small and easy success at a time using laser focus until the ultimate goal is achieved. This is how it is done.

I am so happy and greatful now that I am earning $10,000 a month in passive income.

m   Establish which market to invest in.

m

m

m

m

M

M

M

M $6,000 per month in passive income.

M $8,000 per month in passive income.

$10,000 a month in passive income by July 1st.

To DOS!

1. Google top ten real estate markets.
2. Get mentor's opinion.
3. Call fellow investors for their opinion.
4. Factor in opinions to my own research and make a decision!

Using the power of questions, I have found the use of the following questions in formulating my daily to-do list accelerates my success. Feel free to use them.

1. What about my to-do list excites me today? Why?
2. How will it make me feel once I've crossed it off the list?
3. What is one risk I can take today that will move me even closer to my goal?
4. If I could add one thing to my list that would make a tremendous difference in achieving my goals, what would it be?
5. What skills do I wish to develop to enhance my business?
6. To what activities do I devote too much time which I could eliminate or dramatically reduce?
7. What is the most valuable use of my time, and how can I spend more time doing that?
8. How can I borrow more time from areas that do not serve me?

By incorporating Step 7 daily, staying focused on the small, easy daily activities and checking in with your Minorstones every other week or so, success will be yours. It is the small and easy, sometimes mundane, activities compounded over time that produce success. It can't be any other way. There's no such thing as "get-rich-quick" or "overnight-success." Patience and persistence are what does it, and they win every time.

CHAPTER 10:
WORK THE PLAN

An Ignored Step

"To will is to select a goal, determine a course of action that will bring one to that goal, and then hold to that action till the goal is reached. The key is action."

– Michael Hanson

To this point, you have strengthened your relationship with success, you have removed (or are in the process of removing) the seven toxins that kill success, you've defined your dream, and you have charted the course to your dream's realization. You have created your Major and Minor Milestones. If you're like most, you're feeling really good about this process right now. You are inspired by your Do Over Plan, and you might even be feeling that burn to get started. You have meticulously planned the work, now it's time to unleash that burn and start working the plan. This is where your inspiration is introduced to perspiration. It's time to take action.

Seems simple, yes? Taking action? Simple, absolutely. Easy? Not always. What I mean by that is I have found that people love to learn how to do things, they love to dream about things, they love to even plan things, but they do not love to DO things. They know that they should, and in some weird cases they might even want to do, but they still don't.

Do you know anybody like this? Maybe somebody closer to you than you'd like to admit? Taking action is the most ignored step to producing results. It almost sounds funny, doesn't it? How can anyone expect to produce a result unless they take action? Many do, and it's tragic because in ten to twenty years from now, those who fail to take action will be more disappointed by the actions they didn't take than the actions they did. That's called regret, for which there is no cure. You can dream, believe and plan to your heart's content, but at the end of the day...*nothing happens until something moves.* Neither success nor happiness is even possible without action.

A thought or an idea, of and by itself, has no intrinsic value. It must be accompanied by action, and action is nothing more than a decision. The only thing that stands between you and everything you want is getting off your butt and doing something. It's really that simple.

Take *action*
Not next week, not tomorrow, not even later today
Do it *now*

Never set a goal without taking some form of positive action toward its achievement. You have created your Do Over Plan so you will have a daily list of actions to take, but action can be something really small like making a phone call or shooting off an e-mail. The practice to adopt is to just do something. We'll go into greater detail later on how the little actions are what will make the difference. They are what will get you from where you are now to where you want to be.

In our age of technology and information, sometimes basic actions might not be enough. Rapid action can be required because we no longer necessarily live in a world where the strong beats the weak, the big beats the small.

Today, it's the *fast* that beats the *slow*.

The more that society evolves, the more people come to expect things fast. Economists are calling today's generation the "immediate gratification generation." Regardless of what you are up to in life, you are in the people business. Anything and everything you want, you will have to interact with people to get it. So, respond to the people you interact with quickly. Do everything fast. Taking immediate action in today's age produces not only faster results, it produces better results.

Develop a reputation as someone who follows through and follows through fast. People give their loyalty, their business and favors to those who act and deliver fast. Opportunities rarely come to those who wait; they are captured by those who act fast. Do you get the picture? Fast, fast, *fast!*

Fast? Yes. Careless? No.

Do not get *fast* action confused with *thoughtless* action. I'm not suggesting acting with such haste and flurry that it results in carelessness. There is logic in the idioms "Haste makes waste" and "Look before you leap." We have taken several chapters of this book to carefully plan, but once the plan is in place, get going. While executing your plan, you will find yourself in unexpected situations where you will have to make some quick judgment calls. I've compiled a few power questions to assist you in those calls so that you do not get stopped.

- Is this decision/action fair to everyone involved?
- Does this decision/action move me closer to my goal?
- If this decision/action creates a short-term setback, does it promote long-term growth?
- Is anyone being hurt by this decision/action?

Getting out of the starting blocks quickly will attract people's attention and ignite momentum, but there is more to do. At the end of the day, what counts is where you are when the race is over. Quick, consistent and persistent action takes discipline, and discipline is what wins the race. Consistent and persistent action is where many people really miss the boat. For the next two years, if you work your Do Over Plan with discipline (which most people won't do), you will be able to do for the rest of your life what most people can't do – and that is my definition of freedom.

The word "discipline" is more commonly associated with the idea of work, duty and actions we should do rather than with the idea of freedom. We think of discipline, whether self-imposed or imposed by another, as consistent, orderly actions that move us toward a goal. Rarely do we connect the idea of freedom with a term like "should." Freedom is doing what we want, right? In the world in which we live, access to that type of freedom comes through discipline. True freedom is synonymous with disciplined action. It is necessary to comprehend this on such a deep level in order to perceive that disciplined action is imperative to such freedom. It bears repeating: if you work your Do Over Plan with discipline for the next two years (what most people won't do), you will be able to do for the rest of your life what most people can't do. You will be living your dream, and you will be free.

CHAPTER 11:
FLEXIBILITY

It will take discipline to work your plan to its end – and discipline takes strength and stamina. If you expect to realize your dreams, you will have to be persistent and unyielding in your pursuit of them. Specifically, it will take a special kind of strength. I took martial arts when I was a kid, and I remember the *sensei* referencing a Bruce Lee quote: "Notice that the stiffest tree is most easily cracked, while the bamboo or willow survives by bending with the wind." The strength and resilience of the bamboo tree is legendary, and its strength was apparent when many trees survived the atomic bombs of Hiroshima and Nagasaki with minimal damage. What you'll want to take from this is to be strong in working your plan, yet be flexible.

It should be of no surprise that the world isn't going to deliver on a silver platter everything you need to achieve your goals. Improvising, adapting, and overcoming obstacles are normal, and are to be expected when working your plan. The fact that our dreams aren't going to be just handed to us is precisely why achieving them require us to live outside our box, be somebody we haven't been before, and stretch our thoughts and ideas to new dimensions as to what we perceive as possible.

Our Creator Tests Us

Regardless of your faith, I believe tests are sometimes given to us by a Higher Power. Mine is God. I believe He frequently tests our belief and faith in Him. Acknowledge His tests for what they are, just tests.

Don't fail your tests. Maintain focus on your dream.

I'll say it again and again and again:

Your dream must be big enough to move you through the tests.

Understand that tests and obstacles are simply part of the game. Rather than focusing on the tests and obstacles, focus on the solutions that will enable you to overcome them. Every test and obstacle has a solution. Often it will take flexibility in what you've known to be true in the past to solve the problems you encounter. If not, they typically wouldn't be problems.

Don't get discouraged. Be flexible.

– Matt Theriault

Just like the Apollo 11 mission to the Moon was off course 97% of the time, the same is true with a plane flying from Los Angeles to Hawaii. Without flexibility and adjustments, the plane would never reach its destination. The trip to your destination will work just like that. As a plane has its instrument panel to keep it on course, you have your emotions, intuition, the power of questions and your faith to keep you on course. Trust yourself and know that adjusting is normal and it's part of the journey.

Don't get discouraged. Be flexible.

CHAPTER 12:
CREATE A GAME

An Unknown Step

"If life doesn't offer a game worth playing, then invent a new one."

– Anthony J. D'Angelo

Imagine yourself sitting on a park bench, and you notice in the distance a group of teenagers playing at the basketball court. It would be very easy to discern if they were playing a game or just goofing around. The mere action and intensity of their movements would suggest whether or not they were keeping score.

Human beings respond well to games.

Action persists.

Intensity increases.

Motivation lasts.

Most of all, games are *fun*. When fun is present, so is focus – sustained focus. I previously referenced the power of focused energy. When our focus is clear and sustained, we can do anything. I have found that by creating a game around the pursuit of my most important goals, and keeping score within that game, this method both accelerates my progress and increases the probability of achievement.

If you can't measure it, you can't manage it. Previously, we established Major and Minor Milestones, which are one form of measurement. These milestones, when reached, let us know that we're getting closer to our goal. However, the time spent in between milestones can vary greatly, and when that time exceeds our expectations, emotions like frustration, discouragement, and doubt can attack us. These emotions can be toxic to our success. The Major and Minor Milestones will keep us abreast to how close we're getting to our goals, but they don't do much for supporting the probability of their achievement.

To clarify, let's stick with the basketball analogy for an example. Imagine a high school basketball team's goal is to win the state championship. In order to get there, the team must first win the city championship, the county championship and then the regional championship. Those would be their Major Milestones. There will be a number of games to be played in between each championship that must be won to progress; those would be the team's Minorstones. As you can see, the milestones, major and minor, keep the team abreast as to how close they're getting to their goal of a state championship.

Micro Milestones (Microstones)

What's missing, however, is a measurement that supports the probability of getting to the championship. In this analogy, that would be the daily routine the team conducts in between games. Activities like practice, conditioning, nutrition, and rest. The activities can be broken down to very specific actions, or daily habits if you will. I refer to these as Microstones. Specifically, they are the few activities that have the most impact on the probability of you reaching your goal. In our basketball example, a Microstone may be free throw completions during practice. There are a certain number of free throws a player must shoot in practice on a daily basis to develop the skill that contributes to the team winning. There are a certain number of laps a player must run in practice on a daily basis to develop the stamina that contributes to the team winning. There's a certain diet a player must maintain on a daily basis to maintain his or her health that contributes to the team winning. These are three specific activities that have the most impact on determining the probability of whether a player will contribute to his team winning or not, and they can be measured.

The true secret to success really is **mastering the mundane**. Yes, the secret to success is mastering the mundane. The word "mundane" doesn't sound fun to me; and I know if it's not fun, action dwindles, intensity wanes, motivation ebbs, and most of all focus disperses. Energy dispersed has no power and produces minimal, if any, results.

Enter the game!

Your goal is now the state championship.

- Your **Major Milestones** are now the city, county, and regional championships.
- Your **Minorstones** are now the individual games.
- Your **Microstones** are the daily activities that measure the likelihood of you reaching the next milestone, and you will measure them with points and a daily scorecard.

You will focus on the few activities that have the most impact on reaching your milestones and assign them a point value. You've certainly heard the cliché, "Focus on one day at a time," yes? It's amazing how much power there is in clichés (perhaps that's the title of my next book – *The Power of Clichés?*). When it comes to reaching your goals and achieving your dreams, focusing on one day at a time is key. Rome was not built in a day (oops, another cliché). Do not focus on the end result. Do not focus on the state championship. Focus on the activities that will produce the end result. Focus on the daily activity of shooting free throws, and count them. Keep score. It's important, no, it's vital to know at every moment if you are winning or not. To do so, create a daily scorecard. A daily scorecard maintains activity, intensity and motivation. It drives planning and course correction so that your goals and dreams are not perpetually goals and dreams, so that your goals and dreams are achieved.

Like the teenagers playing basketball in the park, we only get serious when we start keeping score. Keeping score creates a game, a game arouses competition, and competition gets things done. A game gives you a framework in which to accomplish new things, things you never thought possible for you.

What there is to do next is to identify what daily activities, repeated consistently over time, will measure the probability of you reaching each Major Milestone, and ultimately your goal. Using my $10,000 a month of passive income goal as an example, I keep a daily scorecard of how many properties I analyze each day.

✓ I give myself 1 point for each property I analyze.

✓ I track how many purchase contracts I write a day, and I give myself 2 points for each contract.

✓ I track how many escrows I open a day, and I give myself 3 points for each opened escrow.

✓ I track how many escrows I close a day; I give myself 4 points for each closed escrow.

I'm so happy and grateful now that I'm earning $10,000 a month in passive income.									
	1	2	3	4	5	6	Sub Total	Points	Total
Property Analyzed	X	X	X	X	X	X	6	**x1**	6
Offers Written	X	X	X				3	**x2**	6
Escrow Opened	X						1	**x3**	3
Escrow Closed	X						1	**x4**	4
								Total Pts.	19

I know if I score 15 points per day, I will eventually win the state championship. Every day you should come home feeling like you are "getting there," making progress, instead of getting stressed out about how much further you have to go. I take great solace, and you will too, knowing that I get closer to manifesting my dreams and goals every day by simply tracking and scoring my Microstones. The scoring virtually eliminates the frustration, discouragement and doubt that used to appear for me in between each Major Milestone.

If your goal is to be the #1 salesperson in your company, you may want to create a daily scorecard for, and assign points to, the number of new prospects you speak with, the number of appointments you set, the number of presentations you give, and the number of products you sell. If your goal is to win your company's golf tournament, you may want to create a daily scorecard for, and assign points to, the number of golf balls you hit at the driving range, the number of putts you take on the practice green, and the number of times you meet with your golf instructor. If your goal is to lose weight, you may want to create a daily scorecard for, and assign points to the number of…wait…I believe Weight Watchers already has something like this? Yes! Do you know anyone who has lost weight using the Weight Watcher's food scoring system? If you do, did they gain their weight back? If they did, ask them if they stopped using their daily scorecard. Creating a game and keeping score can be a great motivator and be very effective, and it was one of the missing ingredients my first time around. Perhaps it will make the same difference in the pursuit of your goals as well.

One note about creating a game around your goal: it's *your* game. You know your situation better than anyone else, and you will know how to create a game that motivates you into daily action. It's your game. You get to create the rules. Stay focused on your game. Paying undue attention to other people's games will slow you down. Don't compare yourself, it's very limiting. Every moment spent worrying about whether or not someone else is winning their game is a moment wasted on moving forward. I have found that time spent studying others, their games and their scores isn't intelligence gathering as much as it is a search for excuses.

Play YOUR game.

CHAPTER 13:
PLEDGING

An Unknown Step

You now have all the information you will need to accomplish anything you set your sights on. Everything I will share in this chapter and forward are techniques, strategies, technologies, and best practices I have discovered and used to eliminate barriers, lower resistance, and propel me toward my goals with extreme ease and high velocity.

The Pledge

It's not some magical concept or word I've chosen to redefine for the purpose of branding the technique within the Do Over Plan. I'm referring to the word in its most literal sense. To pledge is to deliver something as a security for the fulfillment of a promise, something that is subject to forfeiture if you fail to fulfill the promise. When creating a new goal, I will typically make a pledge inside of that goal, placing my word or reputation on the line. By doing so, I always experience a "supercharging" of sorts; it puts me in a position where I must succeed. It's a higher level of commitment, and calls me into a higher level of performance. Making a pledge prior to embarking on the road to your goals acts as a catalyst that launches you, and your life, into a new level of being. You are now accountable. You are the resource. You are now the key element in achieving the goal to which you pledged.

An analogy I use frequently to create clarity around the concept of pledging is planning a vacation to Paris. There are two ways to go about planning a vacation to Paris. One way is to first plan the vacation and then purchase the plane ticket. The other way is to first purchase the plane ticket and then plan the vacation. By purchasing the plane ticket first, you will get to Paris more often than if you had planned first. By purchasing the plane ticket first you will get to Paris with greater ease, and often times your vacation will be accompanied by unexplainable, yet fortunate happenstance.

The moral is to always purchase the plane ticket before you start planning. It significantly increases the likelihood of a successful trip, and it somehow causes the universe to conspire in your favor, producing a greater vacation than you had originally envisioned for yourself. The phenomena behind purchasing the ticket first works for manifesting your dreams and goals in precisely the same way it does in producing a successful vacation to Paris. So, buy the ticket! Or, when it pertains to your goals...make a pledge!

One of the more notable pledges in history came from U.S. President John F. Kennedy. In 1961, JFK stood before the American people and promised a man would land on the Moon and return safely within the decade. The resources and talent to accomplish the task were believed by JFK to be in place, but a plan or idea of how it would be accomplished was not. JFK made a pledge, and because he did, the universe immediately began to conspire in his favor. On July 20, 1969, almost six years after JFK's death, Neil Armstrong set foot on the Moon and uttered the famous words, "That's one small step for man, one giant leap for mankind." The irony in this example is that pledging can literally produce "giant leaps" toward your goals.

JFK was not the first to demonstrate the pledge. The concept has its roots in Irish folklore. As the story goes, there were two Irish lads on their way somewhere when they found their path obstructed by a wall too high to scale. As the two boys pondered their dilemma, staring at the presumably insurmountable obstacle, they concluded the first step was to renew their commitment to their destination. In unison they removed their caps and tossed them over the wall. To retrieve their caps, they had to scale the wall – and they did. The expression "Throw your hat over the wall" was born. My mom has a different expression. She calls it how she sees it: "Put your ass on the line." By throwing your hat over the wall, external forces begin to work with you. For example, with your hat on the other side of the wall, you may start to think differently than you would've if you had not thrown it over. This different thinking could result in you inventing a new type of trampoline to bounce you over the wall, or the idea of calling someone you haven't thought of in years who could give you a boost over the wall.

What I have found to happen more often, however, is the unexplainable. The unexplainable may show up in the form of a stranger walking by who just happens to have a key to a door in the wall and allows you to walk through, or you accidentally trip over a shovel that allows you to dig a tunnel under the wall, or for no reason at all a rope is tossed over from the other side by someone you don't even know. Don't ask me how or why pledging works; just know it works every time (or it is in the process of working) for me – and I'm confident it will work for you.

My Goal-Setting Workshop

I have experienced this positive phenomena several times in my life, and the time that immediately comes to mind is the very first time I deliberately put it to the test. Looking to conquer a personal fear of public speaking, I put pledging to the test. I decided to create an event where I would be the focus of attention and forced to speak in front of as many people as possible. Being a real estate agent at the time, I sent an e-mail to my broker that I wanted to host a goal-setting workshop for my fellow real estate agents. I had never done anything of the sort and had no idea what a goal-setting workshop even looked like, but I sent the e-mail to my broker and gave her the date, which was two weeks away. I made my pledge.

A goal-setting workshop is obviously not in the realm of putting a man on the Moon, yet the elements are similar. I declared something, gave it a deadline, and had no idea as to how it would be accomplished. My broker accepted my invitation. A week went by and I had done nothing to prepare, and I had heard nothing from my broker. The idea of the workshop now didn't seem as good as it did when I thought of it, and I was actually hoping my broker had forgotten. A few more days passed and still no word from my broker, and my mind was now on other things. I was certain she had forgotten.

On the day before the workshop, my broker's assistant called and asked me if I needed anything special for the workshop. The assistant went on to inform me that many agents, including the broker herself, were planning to attend and the excitement within the office was building.

Have you ever had that feeling when you feel like you just swallowed your heart? I began to panic. I had absolutely nothing planned, and in twenty-four hours I was to conduct a goal-setting workshop for fifty real estate agents.

I assembled an outline for my workshop and created an acceptable Power Point presentation. I was up until 3:00 AM the night before, but I did it – and the workshop was a success.

There are forces that come together for the greater good when making a pledge. One of those forces is *accountability.* If I had not made a pledge to my broker, it would've been very easy for me to blow it off. But I did make the pledge, and I had to perform.

A result that often appears after making a pledge and then achieving a goal is that *the outcome is greater than what you had expected.* For example, prior to that workshop, becoming a coach, a mentor, or a professional public speaker was nowhere in my life's plans. Writing a book wasn't in the plan for at least another decade, yet it was that workshop that gave birth to the idea of writing this book now and an additional career as a business coach, public speaker, and author. If I hadn't made that pledge, I would not be enjoying the rewarding life that I am now. I would've completely missed out on the countless relationships I've built and growth I've experienced. I don't even resemble the person I was prior to that goal-setting workshop. In my opinion, by making that small e-mail pledge to my broker, my accomplishments and personal growth have been dramatically accelerated by at least ten years.

Pledging to Build in the Lower Ninth Ward

There is great power in pledging. As I am writing this book, I have implemented the power of pledging in a much bigger project than a goal-setting workshop. In 2005, I was deeply affected by the stories and images associated with the destruction of Hurricane Katrina. I remember it like it was yesterday – I couldn't believe the images of destruction, despair, and death I saw on TV. "Those are Americans in America in need; why isn't anyone helping them?" I remember saying out loud in a house all by myself.

In the ensuing months and years, the availability of affordable housing emerged as a critical need in South Louisiana. Over 200,000 homes had been destroyed by the category-five hurricane. Demand for housing in the area steadily increased, making it substantially more difficult for South Louisiana's displaced residents to return home. Other than by my own selfish pursuits of time and money freedom, I don't remember ever being so powerfully moved to take action in support of a cause. It has just never been in me to do something of that nature, to help complete strangers. In contrast, the terrible attack of 9/11 certainly affected me and sparked massive rage within, but the idea of doing something about it seemed futile. It seemed way too big, and what could I possibly do to make a difference? I'm just one person. But after a few years of soul searching, personal inquiry, and growth, when Hurricane Katrina hit I was ready. I wanted to do something, and I *believed* I could do something.

Yet as the months went by I did nothing. It wasn't until I heard that story about Gandhi and Martin Luther King, Jr., wishing they had dreamed bigger, and I recognized the concept of pledging – it was no coincidence I learned of these two in the same day – did I take action. My decision was only strengthened a few days later while waiting in line for my "grande drip" at Starbuck's, where I noticed a quote by JFK on a coffee mug, "One person can make a difference, and everyone should try."

I made the decision to contribute housing and teach financial literacy to the worst hit area of New Orleans, the Lower Ninth Ward. I had no idea how I was going to do it because I was in difficult financial shape and uncertain if I would be able to keep my own house, let alone buy a house for someone else. But I made the decision. I decided I would begin by giving one house away by implementing a duplicatable system of creating income that others could easily follow. I would document my progress and publicize it in a way that America would be touched, moved, and inspired to follow suit. In the spirit of the movie _Pay It Forward_, my goal was to inspire just two people to do the same. Those two people would each inspire two people, those four would each inspire two more, those eight would each inspire two more, and so on, until the Lower Ninth Ward was completely rebuilt.

But it had to start with one house. At this point, I had only a vague idea of how this would be accomplished, but I knew I had to make my pledge and throw my hat over the wall. I decided I would give the first house away through an elementary school essay contest. The idea of a child winning a house for their family was inspiring to me, not to mention just plain neat. I would find a school in the Lower Ninth Ward and conduct an essay contest in which the students could participate. However, I wasn't even sure if a school existed. I had never even been to the Lower Ninth.

The next day, my then wife opened a copy of *People* Magazine celebrating "America's Heroes of 2007" and saw that Doris Hicks, the principal of the Martin Luther King, Jr., Charter School for Science and Technology, had been named one of the Heroes of 2007. Her school was in the Lower Ninth.

This was the magic rope tossed over the wall from the other side, and recognizing it as such, my wife immediately called the school, spoke with Mrs. Hicks, and made our pledge. We proceeded to e-mail an outline and rules of the essay contest and had the school's staff read them to the students. We made our pledge to Doris, the school's staff and the students. My hat was officially over the wall, and now I had to go get it.

A month or so passed and we called the school to check in on the progress of the contest. We were staying engaged. When we checked in with Doris, she shared with us some recent developments. The students had voted my wife and I as recipients of their Drum Major for Education award, Principal Hicks had told a major network TV reporter about what we were up to and that the reporter wanted to cover our story.

At this point, I had not raised one dime yet, nor did I even have an extra dime of my own to donate to my own cause. What I want to draw your attention to are some of the forces that began to work in my favor after making a pledge. *As you are executing your daily activities moving toward your goal, your goal is moving toward you.* If I would've reached out to a TV reporter to cover my story before I had done anything, I most assuredly would have been turned away. But because I had made my pledge first, the TV reporter was waiting for me. I could go on and on with examples, but I trust you are starting to see the power in pledging.

> ### As you are executing your daily activities moving toward your goal, your goal is moving toward you.
>
> *– Matt Theriault*

By making a pledge to your dreams (and making it a practice), you will experience the raw thrill of life. You will experience living for a purpose – living for something worthy of your attention, faith, efforts, adversities and triumphs. You will be called to, and you will answer to, new levels of performance. Almost instantly after making a pledge, life shows up as if it matters. Until you throw your hat over the wall and declare that you will find a way, even when a way seems impossible, it is my opinion that you will never know the full power of making a pledge. It gives you life.

By the way, as of the writing of this book, I have yet to fulfill on my pledge of contributing a house to the contest winner from the Dr. King Charter School. The contest is complete, a winner has been chosen, and my dream of making a difference in the Lower Ninth Ward is waiting for me. I spent some time in sharing this with you to renew my pledge, to make a promise to you that I will fulfill on this pledge. To check in on my progress, I invite you to visit http://RebuildTheBayou.org.

Pledging can be a very scary practice. Once making a true pledge, you are fully accountable. You are a resource. You are the key ingredient in manifesting your dreams. Let go of your fear. Trust yourself. You are more powerful than you can imagine.

CHAPTER 14:
FINDING YOUR MENTOR

The concept of working with a mentor makes logical sense: find someone who has done, or preferably is currently doing, what you want to do, and learn from them. At the very least, it helps to have someone to look up to, if for no other reason than to assure you that your goals are indeed attainable. Until you actually are able to experience the power a mentor brings to the table, however, it will always be an underestimated step in producing results. Nothing can create the true understanding and value of the mentor like the mentor experience itself.

After you have defined your dreams and declared your commitment, finding a mentor should be the next thing on your to-do list. Do not ignore or underestimate this step. Get a mentor. Get several if you can, but at least get one. Hire one if you must. There is a Buddhist proverb that says, "When the student is ready, the master appears."

Do not wait for the master to appear – seek the master out. Now!

There are very few things that will contribute more to your success than a mentor. I am convinced of this because I have experienced the power of a mentor first hand, and if I were to share everything that that relationship provided for me, this book would be twice as long as it is. Simply put, I accomplished more in a year with a mentor than I did in the previous five years without one. How is that for collapsing timeframes?

Specifically, during the past twelve months I have had two mentors. The first showed me what "work" looks like, what training and continued education look like, what focus looks like, and how to build a system. The second showed me what "just do it" looks like – the power of "now."

For twenty years I had been an entrepreneur, figuring it out on my own, and had never really witnessed what "work" looked like. I had never understood, I mean truly understood, words like "vision," "focus," and "intention." My mentors gave me that, and nobody can ever take that away from me.

I now share those lessons with others as a mentor myself. In addition to finding a mentor as soon as possible, you will want to become one. Mentoring and teaching are two of the most rewarding practices a human can experience. Not only will you receive an overwhelming sense of empowerment and contribution from mentoring, you will develop a deeper understanding of what you teach and the bolstering of your belief system like nothing else can provide.

I don't want to get ahead of myself. If you don't have a mentor right now, you must find one, and I want to help you do that. I recommend you seek out someone you admire who has the attitude, character, and life you desire, and begin by modeling your behavior after that person. You will want to seek out "tough love" and criticism.

Be Coachable

Seeking praise is useless. If you ask enough people, approval is readily available. It takes no effort at all to find people who will tell us what we want to hear. Consider the time-honored question, "Does this dress make me look fat?" If your mentor is someone who would say, "No, you look fine," he or she is not a good candidate. In fact, don't even consider it.

Now, imagine if your mentor could say, "No, the dress doesn't make you look fat. Your fat makes you look fat. You are fat!" That's your mentor!

That is the type of response that will cause you to grow. Welcome it. Be coachable. Give your mentor the permission to demand the best out of you. In Chapter 9 you should have created a goal big enough that you would be willing to step outside of your comfort zone and allow someone else to contribute. Being coachable is a learned skill that will serve you on the road to success. Use the criticism to drive you. It will take some humility to receive the criticism and feedback. It will take wisdom to understand it, analyze it, and appropriately act on it. When I first began to interact with my mentor, I became more than coachable; I surrendered to his ways. Whether I agreed or not, whatever he said, I did; and because I did, I moved forward with greater velocity than I ever would have on my own.

When seeking out your mentor, you will be surprised how willing people will be to lend a helping hand once they realize you have made a commitment to your dreams and goals. Many people will want to help you, and in turn, you will inspire them. Keeping that in mind, maintain high standards for your mentor because you will encounter two types of people in your quest: advisors and mentors. Advisors *know*, but a true mentor *knows* and *does*. Seek out the doers, and don't be afraid to seek out and work with the best.

The best people can be difficult to find and difficult to get next to. They may be so focused on their own goals that they do not have the time to take on a pupil. That focus is what makes them who they are. This is who you are looking for. They can be intimidating, especially to the young, but if you are fortunate enough to come across this type of mentor, do not get discouraged. If you approach them with a good attitude that conveys you want to do something well, they typically respond positively. Be prepared to run some errands and work for free. You will get a lot of distance out of being proactive and taking initiative while working with your mentor. Don't be the guy (or girl) who says, "Can I just follow you around for a day?" Don't be a cling-on; be of value to your mentor. You may have to present yourself to your mentor as someone of value before you ever get their attention. Expect nothing in return other than the experience of working alongside the person you want to become. That type of experience is invaluable.

Having said all of that, it is good to respect, observe, and learn from your mentor, but do not worship them. Always maintain the belief that you can surpass your mentor and that you can be bigger and go beyond. Those who harbor the sidekick mentality or second-best attitude are invariably second-best doers.

The realization of your biggest dreams really begins once you have found a mentor who believes in you. You can eliminate decades of frustration with the right mentor, one who tugs, leads, and pushes you to knock down milestones one after the other, occasionally landing some jabs of reality and every once in a while delivering a right-hook called "truth." If you find yourself having exhausted your resources for quality mentors and you feel you have no place else to look, I invite you to visit http://VirtualMentorship.com where I have assembled possible mentor candidates for you from every walk of life. Maybe your mentor will be there, maybe not. Considering how important the right mentor is to your success, I recommend you leave no stone unturned.

CHAPTER 15:
MASTERMIND

The term "overnight success" is used to describe a successful person who apparently came from nowhere. However, it often takes only a cursory investigation to reveal there was nothing "overnight" about their success at all. Aside from winning the lottery (if you call that successful), I would say the overnight success doesn't exist. However, the most powerful practice you can inject into working your plan that would create the potential for an overnight success is the practice of masterminding.

Masterminding is coordinating the knowledge, effort and resources of two or more people to achieve a specific goal.

If more people implemented the practice, there wouldn't be so much demand for "How to Be Successful" books. If done correctly, it is that powerful.

Through a properly chosen and conducted mastermind group, I would feel very comfortable in saying your goals are halfway achieved simply by its mere existence. There are two inherent qualities within the mastermind that cause this to be so.

1. The first characteristic is economic in nature. By surrounding yourself with the wisdom, effort, and resources of a group willing and able to lend authentic assistance, obvious economic advantages are available.
2. The second characteristic, for lack of a better word, is almost spiritual in nature. When two minds are brought together for a specific purpose, it's as if a third contributing mind is created.

One of my most valued relationships (and it took me almost twenty years to locate such a person) creates a third mind every time we talk. It's almost as if we carry around a third person in our pocket. My entire adult life I have been a big-idea type of guy, and I always had to sell people on my vision. I'm fortunate enough now that I've been able to surround myself with a handful of powerful minds so that when I have an idea and I share it with the group, it always comes back to me bigger, and often times seemingly easier to accomplish, than it was when I originally thought of it. That's an example of a properly selected and functioning mastermind group.

If you were to analyze the background of any person who has accumulated great wealth and success, you would find they have implemented, consciously or unconsciously, the mastermind practice. I'm sure there are some, although I don't know of any, who have achieved great success on their own. If there is such a person, their road to that success would have been infinitely easier and faster with a mastermind group. The power available through the mastermind group is unattainable through any other practice. This is what makes the practice an underestimated step – people fail to truly understand the power and the speed of the results available.

CHAPTER 16:
FEAR IS YOUR FRIEND

Through one of my mentors, I've come to know fear as exactly what it is 99.9% of the time: False Evidence Appearing Real. Although I can't think of any fear I've experienced as being real, I'm sure there's an exception, so I left the .1% open to satisfy that exception.

Because it deserves the attention, in this book I address the subject of fear not once but twice. Fear is what stands between you and everything you want from life. Once you get a complete understanding that there's nothing to fear but fear itself (it's a shame this quote has become such a cliché because it's one of the great truths), the world will magically begin to open up and present itself as your playground.

I'm a big believer in the notion that we get what we focus on. You can focus on what you fear may happen, or you can focus on what you want to have happen. Not only does action produce results, it cures fear.

Conversely, inaction, indecision, and procrastination fertilize fear.

The complete mastery of fear may or may not be attainable, but the closer you get to being its master the easier life gets – and for that reason alone, mastery of fear is worth pursuing. I have gotten to the point where as soon as I feel fear, I feel an *opportunity for growth*. Each and every time I have acknowledged fear and pushed through that fear, I have experienced amazing emotions of triumph. I have become more connected to fear in the sense that I recognize everything I want is just beyond it. Rewards lie just on the other side.

Fear now *inspires* me into action. I use fear as a tool.

You can do the same. Try this as a discipline. Whenever you are faced with something that scares you, acknowledge it, then do it.

That's the rule. I'm scared, now act. Don't question it. Just do it. Put this discipline into action. And remember, hesitation only enlarges, magnifies, and intensifies the fear. Take action swiftly. Be decisive. Face your fears with action and you control your fears.

Undoubtedly, you will ask yourself after the fact, "What was I scared of?"

Let me write that again: you will ask yourself after the fact, "What was I scared of?"

From that point forward you control that fear, and it will never stop you again. Some fears may have to be faced repeatedly before they entirely disappear, but they will disappear. We gain strength, courage, and confidence by each experience in which we really stop to stare fear in the face. You must do that which you think you cannot.

The False Evidence Test

There's an exercise I use to flush out the false evidence within the fear that stops us. I use the exercise in my real estate workshops to get people over the fear of submitting purchase offers for real estate. I call it the *False Evidence Test*. To demonstrate how it works, I'll lead you through the exact exercise I do with my students; however, the exercise will reveal the False Evidence Appearing Real in anything you fear.

To begin, you will need a blank piece of paper and something to write with. Divide the paper into four columns. Title column 1 "Worst Case Scenario." In this column I have my students call on their full imaginations and write down every disastrous result they can think of from making an offer to purchase an investment property in which a $10,000 earnest money deposit is required. The first answer to find its way to column 1 is typically, "The offer gets rejected." Invariably, the second answer is, "The offer gets accepted" and is then followed by group laughter.

Based on the now-expected laughter, it suggests to me that my students fear their offers getting accepted more than they fear them being rejected. They're subconsciously admitting how funny it is to be afraid of the positive outcome. They're afraid of success. It's a common response to laugh at, or make fun of, fears to make them seem like they're not that big of a deal, but they are a big deal, nonetheless. At the end of the day, whether your fears are serious or laughable, they still stop you from taking action. No action, no results. They're all a big deal, and they deserve your attention.

Back to the exercise. I proceed to humor my students and switch the scenario to, "What's the worst-case scenario if your offer was accepted?" I will get basic responses like, the roof is bad, the foundation is bad, the electricity is bad, the plumbing is bad, the financing falls through resulting in losing the earnest money deposit, the property doesn't re-sell, a tenant is nowhere to be found, etc. Then I push them a bit to really employ their imaginations and draw out the worst-case scenarios. I start to get answers like the property is in a flood zone and gets washed away the day after escrow closes, it's built on a toxic waste dump, the neighbor is a made member of organized crime, it burns down, a tornado blows it down, space aliens abduct the property for research, etc. It gets pretty silly by the time we're done with column 1. The point is there is a giant list of what can go wrong, and that's the list we understandably fear and it prevents us from taking action.

On to column 2. Title it "Recovery Time." In this column you will write the time it would take for you to recover if the worst case scenarios actually happened. Meaning, how long would it take to get back to the exact situation you were in just prior to the initial action? In our example that would be the moment just before submitting the offer. Most people say three months to six months. Depending on their financial situation, some will say a year or two, while others will say a couple of days of emotional distress and they would be ready to re-load. Whatever the recovery time would be for you, I'm confident that it wouldn't take very long.

Title column 3 "Risk Management." In this column you will write everything you could've done to minimize the chance of the worst-case scenario ever happening. To stay with our example, a property inspection could've prevented a great deal, putting a second or third financing option in place would've limited risk, negotiating a different earnest money deposit so there was less at risk would've helped, conducting comprehensive research in both the sales and the rental markets, including multiple contingencies in the contract, asking for second and third opinions from people with more experience than yourself, running a police report and buying insurance would've managed the vast majority of atrocities. I'm not sure what could be done about the aliens, but there's a lot that could be done that would virtually eliminate the risk in purchasing an investment property. Almost everything in column 3 can be satisfied by education. This is a perfect example of how "the ultimate invisible barrier," reluctant learning, addressed in Chapter 5 can thwart your success.

Title column 4 "Best Case Scenario." It should be obvious, but in this column you will write the best-case scenario. Using our real estate example, you would get the offer accepted, open escrow, fund the deal, take ownership, execute the exit strategy and earn the desired profit; and perhaps the deal ends up even better than expected, resulting in a bigger profit.

False Evidence Test

1	2	3	4
WORST-CASE SCENARIO	RECOVERY TIME	RISK MANAGEMENT	BEST-CASE SCENARIO
Foundation cracks	Six months	Inspection	Foundation is good
Financing falls through	One month	Due diligence	Financing is good
Built on toxic waste dump	One year	Land use research	No toxic waste
House burns down	Six months	Fire prevention and alarms	No fires

If you were to implement all of the risk management steps in column 3, what would be more likely? The worst-case scenario? Or, the best-case scenario? Without a doubt, the best-case scenario! Unfortunately, it's everything in the worst-case scenario column that stops us from taking action. It's the "false evidence" that stops us over and over and over. It doesn't matter what it is. Visit http://theDoOverGuy.com to view a video of this exercise.

To further illustrate how silly we can be when it comes to our fears, you'll find that "death" is almost never a worst-case scenario. Yet, every day we engage the #5 killer in the United States without giving it a second thought. Do you know what that killer is? If you guessed an automobile, you're correct. Why do we get in a car on a daily basis with death lurking at every intersection, and yet we won't speak in public, we won't approach the opposite sex, we won't ask our boss for a raise, we won't start that business we've been dreaming about and we won't participate in the most lucrative industry in the world, real estate investing? The answer is very easy. When we drive an automobile we have learned to *manage our risk*. We've implemented everything that would be in column 3 if we conducted the false evidence exercise with driving a car. We keep both hands on the steering wheel, we keep our eyes on the road, we obey the speed limit, we stop at the red light, we go at the green, we change the oil, rotate the tires, maintain the brakes, and we've repeated the process hundreds, if not thousands, of times.

Imagine if you could create wealth through real estate investing as easily and efficiently as you drive a car. To gain ultimate time- and money-freedom, would it be worth managing that risk and conquering that fear? If so, I invite you to visit my real estate "risk management" website at http://EpicProfessionals.com, and I'd be glad to help you take the next step. If not, no worries. Remember this exercise will work for whatever you aspire to.

> Recognize fear as your friend from this day forward, and you will transform your life and miracles will be yours.
>
> *– Matt Theriault*

Using this exercise, I have conquered the fear of public speaking, raising private money, cold-calling, and being direct in my communication with friends and family. With just a few fears eliminated from my life, I hardly recognize myself from as little as a year ago. Recognize fear as your friend from this day forward, and you will transform your life and miracles will be yours.

CHAPTER 17:
COMMUNICATION AND SHARING

"Language creates reality" is a concept I embrace more by the day. Specifically, I'm referring to the type of communication and sharing that produces results. But for me to convey the power of language, I will need to first lay a foundation for the concept of language creates reality.

For this to make sense, there are two concepts you will need to understand. It's entirely okay if these two concepts are a little "out there" for you; just know that they exist.

The first concept you will need is that "language persists." The second is to understand how your perception of your environment affects your being. Once understood, you can literally speak your results into existence.

Sound waves, regardless of their cause, have an audible beginning and end. For example, if you were to clap your hands together once, an audible result would be produced. A single clapping of your hands would generate a sound wave, and that sound wave has a definite beginning and end. When we speak, there is also a sound wave produced, and it too has a definite beginning and end. However, because language through our speaking is combined with the sound wave, the *result* of the sound wave persists.

Here's what I mean. If I were to compliment you on the nice shirt you are wearing, your brain would process the compliment, likely resulting in an emotion. You would hold that emotion for a period of time (1 second, 1 hour, 1 day, 1 week, or longer) after the sound wave dissipated. To further illustrate the creation, allow me to presume you would feel an emotion of flattery or gratitude from the compliment of your shirt. Those two emotions would likely impact your next words or actions, meaning you may smile, you may respond with thanks, or you may extend a compliment of your own in return. Whatever your next words or actions would be, you could say the initial compliment of your shirt produced them, or at the very least influenced them.

Conversely, an insult to your shirt would also produce a distinct result. In reality, the comment about your shirt consisted only of a sound wave. It had a beginning and an end. The introduction of language to the sound wave, however, caused the result to persist and produce a greater result than just a sound wave. That is one way language can create reality.

We Behave the Way We Are Perceived

Have you ever noticed the difference in your behavior with various groups of people? For example, among your co-workers you may be very polite and professional; around your childhood friends you may be wild and crazy; and in the company of strangers you may be very quiet and reserved. We, as humans, behave in direct correlation with how we perceive the people around us perceive us. The people we interact with give us our being.

For example, your co-workers may perceive you as a straight-and-narrow professional Joe, so you behave as a straight-and-narrow professional Joe in the presence of your co-workers. Your childhood friends know you as a wild-and-crazy Joe, so you behave as a wild-and-crazy Joe in the presence of your childhood friends. The people around us give us our being.

Once you understand how words create reality and that the people around us give us our being, you will develop the power to literally use words with the people around you to create your results and create yourself. Because I have been trained using this distinction, I can intentionally use language as a means to not only create a reality in others, but also myself. In the interest of not losing you in this chapter, I will not take you through the entire training I have experienced to attain this understanding. An entire book could be written on this subject alone. Rather, I will share with you through one story of how I intentionally used language to create my reality. I did it through public communication and sharing.

I have always been reticent and reserved around strangers, and when I got involved in a direct sales company, I wasn't any different. For months I was my typical, quiet self, observing others and my surroundings. If you've ever been involved in a direct-sales, multi-level, or network marketing type company, you will know that an introverted personality is not typically a strength. I got involved with this particular company because I fell in love with the product, an unprecedented real estate investing education program. I wanted to be a real estate investor, and the company product, structure, and environment made sense to me. After immersing myself in the product, I attended one of the company workshops on how to purchase real estate through tax deed auctions. That day I learned two things that lit a fire under me:

1. Purchasing real estate through tax deed auctions is one of the more efficient ways of finding "deals," and
2. The next tax deed auction for my county was only three weeks away.

I was determined to participate.

At the time, I didn't have the $5,000 necessary to register for the auction, so I called a friend – his name is also Matt – and gave him all the details. I explained how thousands of Los Angeles properties were about to go up for auction at literally pennies on the dollar, and that he needed to go down to the County Office and register us for the auction. "Oh, and don't forget to take $5,000 with you." In a few hours my friend and I were successfully registered for the auction.

My friend brought the list of properties home for us to review. We narrowed the list down to 136 properties that met our criteria. We carefully analyzed each property, establishing what our maximum bid would be so that in the worst-case scenario we would produce a $50,000 profit per property. We started doing the numbers and realized, "Wow! If we only get 20 of these 136 properties we will have made $1 million in one day!" Needless to say, that really lit me up.

The last piece of the puzzle was that on the day of the auction we would need a 5% down payment for each property we purchased. We would then have thirty days to fund the balance. I wasn't concerned about finding the rest because based on our market and property analysis, the money would find us if we were disciplined during the auction process and did not exceed our maximum bids. That's how great the deals were.

Knowing that language creates reality, I proceeded to publicly share with anyone who would listen that I was going to generate a million dollars in one day using none of my own money and none of my own credit. I was on a mission, and I invited everyone to come watch me do it. I told family, friends, associates, and even people at the local grocery store and Starbucks. I told people exactly to the "T" how I was going to do it, and extended the offer that I would return 100% on their money in ninety days if they wanted to invest with me.

It was amazing! I had people writing me checks left and right, and on the day of the auction I had people calling in sick to work so they could watch me in action. My language, public sharing, and enthusiastic communication had definitely created a "reality" for me.

Three weeks later my friend and I entered the giant auction hall with my binder of 136 property analyses and $100,000 in a trust account. We were ready to play the game. As I grabbed my seat among the thousand auction participants, I perused the auction program of available properties and to my chagrin, only four (yes – only four) of my 136 properties were still available. I felt like I had just been kicked in the stomach. The entourage that followed me (the ones that had cancelled their plans, called in sick, and made arrangements for babysitters) all noticed my facial expression as I made my way through the auction program. They knew something was wrong. I was direct in my communication, informing the group that there were only four properties of the 136 properties in which to place a bid, and that the million dollars was not going to be, at least not that day. I remember someone saying, "Well, four properties multiplied by $50,000 is $200,000, and that would still be a very successful day." I agreed.

As we sat around waiting for our properties to come up in the auction, I proceeded to share with everybody how diligent I was with my property analysis. I actually gave a small class in property analysis, explaining to them every step of the analysis process and how market value is determined. Sharing my evaluation process was keeping my mind off the huge letdown. The first property was moving up the ladder. Our time to bid was getting close. I was nervous, but I couldn't wait to get the first property.

Our number came up and the auctioneer began. "We will start the bid for property #189 at $6,554," bellowed through the auction hall. Yes! That is not a misprint. $6,554 for a California home, in Los Angeles no less. Are you starting to get the picture of why I was so excited in the first place? I believed for us to make a $50,000 profit on this particular property we could not bid one cent over $97,000. Once again to my chagrin, the bidding skyrocketed in a matter of seconds, well over our maximum bid, and ended up somewhere around $400,000. To myself, and then to the group, I said about the winning bidder, "What an idiot, you can get better deals than that right off the Multiple Listing Service!" The group laughed at my comment, but I was really disappointed not to have won.

The next property came up, and it was almost an exact repeat performance of the first property. The third property, same thing. The fourth property – same! "Are you kidding me?" I thought. "After so much preparation and work, I'm going to walk out of this auction with nothing?" Yep, nothing.

I returned everyone's money with a heartfelt apology and explanation of why there was no profit. I was really upset and embarrassed, but I was also very surprised by the response of my entourage, supporters and investors. Feeling so ridiculous that I had shouted from the rooftops that I was going to make $1 million in one day, I was expecting jeering, ridicule and "I knew it wouldn't work" type remarks.

But to my amazement, I received a newfound respect and reverence from my community. My community had witnessed my enthusiasm, my diligence, my attention to detail, my honesty, and most of all…my willingness to take a shot. They all acknowledged me for getting on the court and playing the game, sticking to my parameters, being responsible and not taking any risks with their money. In a few moments I went from depression to inspiration; my community gave me my being. I appeared to them as a courageous, professional and honest "go-getter." From that day, I was created as such.

Since then, most of those people who entrusted me with their money at that first tax deed auction have backed me in several other endeavors, all of which produced significant returns for them. My sharing and direct communication created an amazing reality for me. It literally launched my Albino Dino (http://AlbinoDino.com) real estate investing company, creating win/win solutions where I come to the aid of distressed homeowners and investors while producing significant returns for those who entrust me with their money.

Sharing Generates Rewards

Always aware of how language creates reality, I am collapsing time-frames and moving forward with astounding velocity in my career, finances, and overall life like I have never experienced before. Recently, I accepted the assignment of raising $1 million for an investment partnership, not having any idea how it would come about other than I would commit to share, and my reality would be created. I give credit for most of my results to my willingness to share what I'm up to with anyone who is willing to listen. The key to sharing that makes all of the difference is that I make a conscious effort to publicly share myself so others can see how my success is possible for them too. That type of sharing gives people confidence and power, and because you now have the understanding of how the people around you give you your being, you understand how that confidence and power you give by sharing is returned to you.

Using this distinction, you can create communities for the sole purpose of sharing possibilities. Sharing gives people confidence and power, and it will come back to you tenfold.

✓ Start networking.

✓ Surround yourself with people, preferably groups (the larger the better), who are open to your vision.

✓ Surround yourself with people who will lift you higher, who live in the world of possibility, who have been there before, and who are smarter than you.

✓ Surround yourself with doers, action takers, and risk takers. Look for honest people and people of integrity, and be sure to include your mentor or coach.

Everything you want out of life you will attain through other people (I believe I have written this a couple of times already). Start creating groups and communities. A place to start may be creating a book club, a mastermind group, or a neighborhood watch group. Maybe start a group where you can position yourself as an authority and teach others? Create a group around one of your passions. Maybe golf, wine, hiking, or underwater basket weaving are one of your passions? Your possibilities and opportunities manifest through communities when you publicly share with them. In fact, your dreams and goals will die without them. With that being so, be intentional about creating quality communities, and share with them.

Do not covet your ideas. Do not keep your dreams, goals, aspirations, and plans a secret. Share everything you know, and more than you give will come back to you. The more you give away the more that is returned to you. You will have multiple experiences where the results produced will almost seem magical, but they're not. Imagine yourself sitting in a bar chatting, talking yourself up, presenting your credentials and ideas. As long as you don't overdo it, you will be perceived as an authority on whatever you shared. But if you surrender to your reticence, you will go unnoticed. Unfair as it may seem, this is the hard cold reality of life. When we are dreaming alone, it is only a dream. When we are dreaming, and sharing that dream, with others, dreams manifest into reality. By implementing communication and sharing in this way, I live in a world where "anything is possible" (and it is). Through your own sharing, the same is available for you.

CHAPTER 18:
FAILURE

If fear is your friend, then failure is your mom and dad. Failure spawns success.

How?

If you haven't failed, you haven't tried.

There is no success without failure.

Before I go further, let me establish that in this book there is no such thing as failure – only feedback.

There is no such thing as a person who is a failure– only a quitter.

Failure is an opportunity to practice your technique and perfect your performance. Failure is nothing more than a condition or fact of producing a less than desirable result or falling short. If you expect to "get it right" the first time every time, you are delusional. Nobody wants to fail, but until you understand and accept that failure is simply a part of the process, the fear of failure will immobilize you. It will literally stop you dead in your tracks. So, accept it.

One quote that forever transformed my entire relationship to failure came from former IBM President Thomas Watson, who said, "If you want to increase your success rate, double your failure rate."

Watson's quote revealed one of my hidden barriers. I noticed in many areas of my life where I hadn't even been trying because I believed I couldn't do it, I would fail. Since receiving this new clarity around failure, I will try anything that's in congruence with my values and the pursuit of my goals. If I fail, so what. I analyze what could have made a difference and try again.

Imagine your relationship to failure as, "So what, try again." What would you choose to do if you knew you would not fail? What would you choose to do if you were completely detached from the outcome, meaning the fear of failure did not exist?

If you find yourself fearing failure, it is because you are attached to the payoff.

At the same time, you will want to know the payoff is always worth the risk. It is more honorable to try and fail than to have never tried at all.

The Four Levels of Learning

The formula for success is to fail, fail fast, and fail often. Perhaps this formula will make more sense when you understand the "Four Levels of Learning" (FLOL). Regardless of what you have learned, are currently learning or will learn in the future, you cannot avoid the FLOL.

1. Level One is referred to as <u>Unconscious Incompetence.</u> This is the level where you don't know what you don't know. To illustrate, I'll use my experience of when I learned how to drive a stick shift. There was a time in my life when I didn't even know what a stick shift was. I was in the first level of learning.

2. At some point by observing my parents drive, I eventually realized what a stick shift was. Although I then knew what it was, I still didn't know how to drive using a stick shift. This is the second level of learning, <u>Conscious Incompetence</u>.

3. Most people spend the majority of their lives in just about everything they do somewhere in between the second and third level. Not until they attempt to "try" will anyone ever get to the third level, <u>Conscious Competence</u>. I remember a few months after my sixteenth birthday, my mother bought me a new red sports car (yes, I was that guy). But it was a bittersweet day. I couldn't wait to get in, pick up some friends, and cruise. The bitter part of the equation was it was a stick shift and I was consciously incompetent at driving one. The only way I was going to learn was to get in the car and do it.

Did I pull out of the driveway the first time in a nice smooth roll? Hardly. If you have ever learned to drive a car with a manual transmission and a clutch, you know what your first time looks like. Did you give up the first time the car stalled? Could that constitute as failure? Did you try again? Did you give up after the second time the car stalled? The third time? Fourth? Likely you didn't. Are there other areas of your life where you gave up after it didn't work, i.e. stalled?

I was so bad at driving that stick shift I was literally unsafe on the road. I didn't let that stop me, though. I would get up at 3:00 AM when there were no cars on the road to go practice, and I did that repeatedly for days. Yes, I was a slow learner. One thing that you'll want to get is that the only way to get from the second level of learning to the third level is by practicing. After a week or so, I was getting the hang of it, but I still had to think about every movement of driving a stick shift. I had reached the third level, Conscious Competence.

4. If practice is what will get you from the second level to the third, what gets you from the third level to the fourth? Perhaps you've heard it referenced as the "mother of learning?" The answer is repetition, massive repetition. The fourth level of learning, Unconscious Competence, is when it becomes second nature. You no longer have to think about it. You just do it. After a month of driving that stick shift, there was no thought at all given to the timing between my left foot on the clutch and my right foot on the gas. It just happened, it was like breathing. What do you do that's second nature, what are you really good at? Playing the guitar? Snowboarding? Knitting? Negotiating? Cooking? Tying your shoes? It doesn't matter what you're good at; you went through the four levels of learning. Whatever you want to take on next, the four levels are waiting for you. There is only one way to get to the fourth level, and that's through lots of failure, practice, and repetition. There are no shortcuts to any place worth going, or anything worth doing.

On an associate's bookshelf I saw the title of one of his books, *You Can't Teach a Kid to Ride a Bike at a Seminar*. I didn't read the book; I didn't feel the need to. The title pretty much said it all. Nobody is going to do it for you. Nobody can just give you the information and then "presto!" you can ride a bike or drive a stick shift. No. You will have to eventually get on that bike and do it yourself. You will crash into walls. You will skin some knees. You will eat some dirt. You will have to fall repeatedly before you can successfully ride that bike.

Plan to Succeed by Failing Often and Quickly

Moving from failure to failure without losing your enthusiasm is much more easily done quickly than it is slowly. Here's what I mean. Imagine you know before you get on that bike for the very first time that you will have to fall twenty-four times before you reach the fourth level of learning. The number "twenty-four" is arbitrary, it will be different for everybody, but for this example your number will be twenty-four. Let's look at three different scenarios.

1. In the first scenario, you plan on practicing riding your bike twice per month and at the end of the year you will have fallen twenty-four times.
2. The second scenario is that you plan on practicing riding your bike four times per month and at the end of six months you will have fallen twenty-four times.
3. The third scenario is that you planned to practice and fall twenty-four times today. Obviously, if you fell your twenty-four times in one day you will have learned quicker than the other two scenarios.

In each scenario you fall twenty-four times, but under each scenario would you be equally good at riding the bike? At the end of the year, under which scenario would you be the best bike rider you could be?

Under the first scenario you fell twice per month, and although at the end of the year you fell twenty-four times and you can ride the bike, you are undoubtedly going to be still pretty wobbly on the bike. The reason being is when you let too much time pass between practice sessions, you essentially start over each time. You forget. The twenty-four repetitions spread out so far apart does not produce the same result as the twenty-four repetitions performed in one day.

The scenario in which you fell twenty-four times in one day produces a far more competent bike rider at the end of the year because you've been competent for 364 days. In the first scenario, you just reached competency (maybe) on the 365th day. In a nutshell, it is easier to learn anything fast than it is slow. Success comes easier fast than it does slow.

The formula for success:
Fail, fail fast, and fail often.

Don't be afraid to fail. Don't let that get in your way. Recognize failure from this day forward as a series of rungs up the ladder, as a success that the details of which have yet to be revealed, as a learning experience, as an opportunity for growth, as a precondition of success. Recognize that most successful people achieved their greatest success only one step beyond what appeared to be their greatest failure. Your biggest strides will follow your long steps back. The person who doesn't experience failure will not experience success.

> I have failed over and over and over again in my life. And that's precisely why I succeed.
>
> – Michael Jordan

Most people, if asked to name nature's most destructive force, would reply with earthquakes, tornados, tidal waves, or hurricanes. But the correct answer is *gravity*. Gravity is responsible for more destruction than anything else Mother Nature has whipped up. The reason is that gravity is persistent. It never gives up. It's not how many times you get knocked down that matters, it's how many times you get up. If you fail to get up, gravity will have gotten the best of you, too.

Regardless of how disastrous your own failures may seem, recognize it's only a snapshot in time. It is never as bad as it seems, never; and there's always tomorrow. Nothing is forever. Your struggles and setbacks will pass, and the best is always to come. It is vain and nonsensical to take life and ourselves too seriously. After all, none of us are getting out alive. We've all heard the expression, "One day we're going to look back and laugh about this." If that's the case, why not now? Life is short. Don't allow failure to compromise the beauty of the journey. Enjoy it. Laugh. Those who laugh, last.

The greatest words ever uttered on the subject of failure come from Michael Jordan. I'm inspired every time I read or hear them. Even if you've heard them before, they bear repeating. It cannot be said or documented enough. "I have missed more than 9,000 shots in my career. I have lost almost 300 games. On 26 occasions I have been entrusted to take the game-winning shot and I missed. I have failed over and over and over again in my life. And that's precisely why I succeed."

Integrity check. Be true to yourself. When something appears to just not be working, and before deciding to quit and categorize it as a "failure," honestly ask yourself, "Is *it* not working, or am *I* not working?" Occasionally, your guard may drop and you may find yourself B.S.-ing your friends, family, employer, customers, etc. We're human, we all can do it thinking there's no harm, and maybe sometimes there isn't any harm. However, the harm is certain when you start B.S.-ing yourself.

Stubborn persistence may be the missing ingredient that bridges the gap between failure and success for you. As it has been documented countless times (and here's one more time), scientist Thomas Edison, inventor of the light bulb, the phonograph, and 1,091 other innovations, persisted through many failures and is an American icon because he simply never gave up.

In case of emergency, break glass! When all else fails, just prior to giving up, whatever it may be, imagine it being successfully accomplished by someone you really dislike. I recognize this last thought on the subject of failure doesn't come from the world of love and creation, but sometimes you've got to pull out the big guns to get it done. *Don't quit.*

Okay, one more. Just prior to giving up, say this to yourself: "I am about to give up on all of my hopes and dreams because [insert reason]." I dare you to find a good enough reason.

Summed up, if at first you don't succeed... Do Over. Yet! If at first you do succeed... don't act too surprised, either.

CHAPTER 19:

ESTABLISHING YOUR INTENT, CREATING YOUR DAY, AND MAKING LIFE WORK

Now you've got the plan, the tools, the resources and the strategies to manifest your Do Over. I have given you everything you need to accomplish your goals and transform your dreams into reality.

What's next?

Today!

Now!

There's a daily ritual I practice before taking any action. I'll share it with you as an optional step. Some will believe in its power, and others will not. However, I'm not asking you to believe in anything. Maybe this will sit well with you, and maybe it won't. Try it on like that pair of sunglasses I mentioned in Chapter 2. If they don't fit, take 'em off.

I'm speaking of a ritual of prayer and creation, one that establishes and reinforces connection, intention, beliefs, and thoughts. I'm not sure exactly how or why it works, but the practice produces results. For me, I experience a higher power (my higher power being God) at work by implementing this ritual; and there's great debate as to whether the results produced by its practice are spiritual or scientific. An outstanding documentary, *What the Bleep Do We Know!?*, explores this debate in great depth. Entire books have been written on the power of your thoughts, creation, and establishing intention. To go much further into detail on the how or why would certainly take us off in another direction. As we're nearing the end of this book and you're likely bursting at the seams to get started on your Do Over Plan, I will share my ritual with you, and it is up to you whether you want to implement its practice. I strongly recommend that you do, but it's up to you.

Mental Gratitude List

As soon as I awake, I begin each day creating a mental gratitude list. I run through my mind all of the things I am grateful for. I will give thanks for things like my health, my family, my friends, my home, where I get to live; the list can be quite long. We all have so much to be grateful for. You should even be grateful for the challenges, struggles, and trials you currently have because they are only strengthening your character and stimulating growth. If you and everyone you know were to throw all of your problems into one big pile, once you saw what everyone else was dealing with you would quickly snatch up all of *your* problems and take them back. So, be grateful for your challenges, too. An additional benefit of running through your gratitude list is that the emotions of gratitude and fear cannot exist at the same time. Being grateful causes fear to disappear, which allows you to perform. Start the day by being grateful.

Visualize the Day

After expressing my gratitude, I start asking for what I want to happen that day. I frequently ask for a safe and timely arrival to the office, my phone calls to be fruitful and fun, my meetings to be productive, for everyone I encounter today to experience increase, to complete my daily to-do list, and to arrive home relaxed without stress. If you do not ask, you will not receive.

Then, like a movie in my mind, I will visualize the day's events happening exactly as I want them to happen, with great ease and joy. I learned this from a story I read about golf legend Jack Nicklaus. Jack visualizes every golf shot prior to its execution, and more times than not he got what he envisioned. Can you argue with his results? It's probably no coincidence that visualization is a big part of Tiger

Woods' pre-shot routine as well. In very much the same way, I visualize myself successful in my profession, and so I am. I visualize myself providing a useful service to my clients and receiving checks that reflect my full value. An important aspect of visualization is to really feel what you're visualizing. Feel it as if it were happening right now. The subconscious part of the brain cannot distinguish the difference between that which is real and that which is imagined. Visualize yourself as a success, and it will be.

Make Room to Receive

The next step in my ritual (and keep in mind that I'm going through this practice while I'm waking up, exercising, eating breakfast, showering, and getting dressed) is to foster thoughts that I'm worthy of my goals and dreams. I'm not creating thoughts of entitlement, but thoughts that it's okay to receive, regardless of how or from where my wants appear. I ask myself what can I give up or get rid of that no longer serves me to make room for what I want. Nature abhors a vacuum, and by creating space in my life, what I want has the ability to appear, and more often than not, it does.

Work Your Plan

After expressing my gratitude, asking for what I want, visualizing my day, and making room to receive, I simply let go and let God do the rest. There is nothing left to do but work your plan and accept your results. Throughout the day, I will listen to my intuition and I will listen to others' as well. God, the Universe, Mother Nature, whoever it is for you will speak to you throughout the day. It is up to you to listen for it. I listen by monitoring my thoughts and trusting my intuition, my gut and my first inclinations.

Rules to Live By

I would like to share with you some rules I live by that not only make life work for me, they seem to make life work with greater ease, and (for lack of a better word) create a life where miracles occur almost on a daily basis. I understand the word "miracle" has a spiritual connotation to most, but that's not the type of miracle to which I'm referring. Any welcomed result produced that was not conceived by me nor has any explanation to why it occurred is in my definition of a miracle. On any given day, anything can happen, and it seemingly does. I give credit to the following rules for producing my miracles. Again, try them on. If you like how they fit, use them. If not, don't.

Rule #1

Honor your word. At the end of the day, it's all that you have. Your reputation depends on it. Always do what you say you will do. This will gratify some people and astonish the rest.

Rule #2

Be on time. Ninety-percent of success is simply showing up.

Rule #3

Make promises you do not know how to keep, but with every intention of keeping them. Now knowing your language creates your reality, why not be bold in making promises? I say err on the side of being bold.

Rule #4

Receive what is given, even when you don't deserve it. God gives you gifts daily. His gifts may appear as a helping hand from a stranger, money from an unexpected source, or as a blessing disguised as adversity. Life, and everything that comes with it, is a gift. Receive.

Rule #5

Proceed as if anything is possible. It is. What the mind can conceive and believe, it can achieve.

Rule #6

Maintain integrity. Plan the work and work the plan. When all you have is integrity, you have enough. Integrity is the precondition for workability, and workability is the precondition for performance. Integrity produces results.

Rule #7

Life is a game – play it. Not taking life too seriously will allow you to enjoy the journey. If it's not that serious, why play to win? Conversely, why not? Winning is fun.

Rule #8

Be ready for your opportunity when it comes. Never stop learning. Consistently invest in the most valuable real estate in the universe – the six inches between your ears. Discover personal development. Feed your mind and spirit with positive, abundant, limitless thinking, ideas and content. Hone your skills. Practice your craft. Determine the most important skill necessary to be successful at your chosen endeavor and study it voraciously, developing mastery.

So, how long will my Do Over Plan take to complete? When will I see results?

Have these thoughts crossed your mind? I bring them up because they are questions I'm invariably asked at about this time. In a nutshell, results happen when results happen. I'm not being flippant, that's just what's so. I've noticed the people that experience the fastest results have one thing in common: they waste no time worrying about what the other guy is doing. They plan their work and they work their plan. Results are great, and they will happen as long as you stay focused and work your plan. I read a Facebook status one day for my best friend that read, "Don't count the days, make the days count." Perfectly written!

If I've accomplished the intent of this book, I have empowered you with several new tools, the ignored, underestimated and unknown steps to producing results. My request at this time is that you're not so focused on the results, however. Don't be so focused on the results that you fail to enjoy and celebrate the effort and the journey. It really isn't the results that will define your success; it's who you will become along the way. Most unsuccessful people will read right through that last sentence and utter something like, "Hogwash, I want the results." If that's you, I invite you to write me once you have achieved your success and tell me that you're more proud of your results than who you have become.

> If the ax is dull and its edge unsharpened, more strength is needed but skill will bring success.
>
> – Ecclesiastes 10:10

Success is not an event or a destination. It is a journey.

CONCLUSION: MONEY

I was raised in a family that frequently uttered expressions like, "Money doesn't grow on trees," "We can't afford that," and "Do you think I'm made of money?" That last one was my dad's favorite. Can you relate? As I got older, it became increasingly evident that these types of references to money were not unique to my family. Most of the country grew up immersed in the same type of thinking.

My first career, music, had its roots in my teenage fascination with breakdancing and hip-hop music. Being a white kid growing up in the suburbs of "The O.C." during the '80s, interaction with kids my age with similar interests was very limited. After taking a job at my favorite music store in the city, I finally found myself establishing relationships with other teenagers with the same affinity for hip-hop, yet not of middle-class means. After a while, I noticed I often felt ashamed and apologetic of my middle-class upbringing. Like any normal teen, I only wanted to fit in. As if the pigment of my skin wasn't enough to cause me to stand out, so was my "ranking" on the socioeconomic ladder. I remember conversations with my friends, trying to convince them that my family was struggling, too, even though we weren't really.

Somewhere in my mid-twenties when I started my record label, again I went out of my way to prove that I was struggling just to get by. In the beginning it was a struggle, but as they say, "I would put five on it" (embellish). The struggle added credibility to my business, so I thought. As my record label's popularity grew, I began associating with a large community of young hip-hop D.J.s, producers, and singers, as well as rap and graffiti artists. Being involved in the conscious side of hip-hop (as opposed to the "bling" or "gangsta" sides), it wasn't cool to perform your craft for money. It was all about the art. "Be true to the game" was expressed daily, as if making money wasn't being true. It seemed almost taboo to discuss, or make, money. And when my label began to generate some decent revenue, I really didn't know what to do.

In hindsight, I absolutely sabotaged my success. I would spread the money around with reckless abandon in pursuit of the moniker, "The label owner who gives back is the one who cares." I'm not saying there's anything wrong with giving back – I'm a big proponent – but there's a way to do it. I now know that to give back, you must get before you give. Doing the opposite keeps everybody poor, and it keeps the giver in debt.

Given those thirty-some-odd years of negative money conditioning, it's no wonder I found myself dead broke at thirty-four years old, just prior to embarking on my Do Over. It wasn't until I read what in my opinion is a revolutionary book for the poor and middle-class, _Rich Dad Poor Dad,_ that my money mindset began to change. It should be required reading senior year in high school. This is when I was first introduced to the term "passive income" and gained a clear understanding of the difference between an asset and a liability. More on that later.

Are You an Owner or an Employee?

One day on a Los Angeles freeway, I was stuck in traffic behind a car that had a bumper sticker on the back that read: _A job is the biggest killer of financial freedom, what is yours costing you?_ Boy, did that stop me in my tracks. Sure, the message was in jest, or not, but it really caused me to analyze life and money. I think most people in America were raised to go to a good school, get good grades, graduate, and get a good job. That's what the American system does – it teaches us to be _employees._ If I didn't know any better, I would almost think that system was a conspiracy concocted by "the man" in order to maintain a steady production of "servants." Thank God I do know better. Or do I? That debate could probably fill up a separate book on its own.

That bumper sticker message went against everything I was ever taught and believed, yet given my life experience, it struck me as being "right on the money," pun intended. I mean it literally only took me three seconds to figure it out. My friends, family, and associates were either employees or unemployed. The only rich person I had ever known, Finis Conner (co-founder of Seagate Technology), was a business owner. It took me almost thirty-eight years of my life to have such an epiphany, to really figure out "money," and the answer is to not be an employee. Believe that.

I wonder what all of those "artists" are doing today, the ones who convinced me not only is money unimportant, but it's bad. Did they figure it out? Or are they walking around in that same fog most of America is walking in?

Money Is Important

We live in a society in which nothing replaces money in the way that it serves us. It puts clothes on our backs, roofs over our heads, and food in our stomachs. It pays the hospital bills, and it allows us to do all of those same things for our families and loved ones. Money is important.

That epiphany led me to the ultimate decision to no longer participate in the notion that money is the root of all evil. Did you know that quote is a Bible misquote? It doesn't read that anywhere in the Bible. The scripture actually reads, "For the love of money is a root of all kinds of evil." (1 Timothy 6:10). That's a very different meaning. I later learned that the Bible has more scripture supporting the marketplace and making money than it does in opposition. The Bible is replete with very rich people, all of which were blessed by God himself. My intent is not to take you to church; rather it is to demonstrate how society will pull evidence, even distorted evidence, from multiple sources out of context to support the preposterous notions that money doesn't buy happiness, rich people are going to hell, only greedy people get rich, etc. Did you know Ecclesiastes 10:19 reads, "A feast is made for laughter, and wine makes life merry, but money is the answer for everything." Yes, it reads "money is the answer for everything!" My little Biblical tangent here was for the purpose of demonstrating that we've been misled as a society and that money is not evil. There are no Biblical roots in this ideology. The roots are man-made; and likely made by men who don't have any money. Misery loves company.

The opening paragraph in Chapter One of Wallace Wattles' book written in 1910, *The Science of Getting Rich*, says it well:

> Whatever may be said in praise of poverty, the fact remains that it is not possible to live a really complete or successful life unless one is rich. No man can rise to his greatest possible height in talent or soul development unless he has plenty of money; for to unfold the soul and to develop talent he must have many things to use, and he cannot have these things unless he has money to buy them with.

Once accepting that the pursuit of money is not bad, and that it's actually necessary in order to do good in the world, I decided I would learn everything I could on how to make money, and more importantly how to keep it and grow it. After exhaustive research, it was revealed to me that it's much easier to make, keep and grow money than I could've imagined. The "unicorn in the woods" was not a myth, nor elusive. Once you know how to make money, it really is rather simple. Frequently, I'm asked to be followed around by people who want to witness what my typical day looks like. My response is, "You would be very bored if you followed me around. My ritual is very simple, and it would be boring to watch. It's not that exciting."

It's very unfortunate that more of the world's people don't recognize how simple it is to be financially free. I was amazed at some of the statistics I uncovered. Did you know that, according to the U.S. Department of Health and Human Services, 94% of today's sixty-five-year-olds are not prepared to retire? Ninety-four percent! Virtually nobody knows how to make and keep money. Who in the world are the American people taking their financial advice from?

More importantly, from whom are *you* taking your financial advice? Take financial advice from someone who has the amount of money you want. Just because a person has the title "financial planner" doesn't mean they're qualified to plan your finances.

Anyone can put on a suit and tie and tell people to live below their means and invest the difference. If that advice alone worked, more than six-percent of our country would be prepared to retire.

My research led me to the painful realization that I had never received any real financial advice in my life. With the exception of my grandparents' sage wisdom of, "Put something away for a rainy day," I was taught nothing about making, growing and keeping money. Only one percent of our country retires with a net worth of five million dollars or more. We're the richest country in the world, and only one percent of our population, after working for forty years, can be classified as "rich."

The One Percent Club

I began to investigate, and I asked myself, "What is the one percent doing that the other ninety-nine percent are not?" As I learned from my very first Tony Robbins program that "Success Leaves Clues," I thought that if I were to do what the one percent does, I could produce the same results and join this exclusive club. I could then share with the world how simple it actually was to accomplish and then they could do it, too. That was the thought, so I proceeded to investigate the wealthy one percent. I found of this small group that ten percent were doctors and lawyers, ten percent were presidents and CEOs of major corporations, five percent were sales people, and one percent made it to the "one-percent club" by way of inheritance or lottery winnings. Not necessarily to my surprise, but seventy-four percent made it to "rich" status by way of business ownership (à la my family's friend, Finis Conner) and real estate investing.

So, this turned out to be a fairly easy decision of what my Do Over would consist of. At age 37, committing the next decade to medical school or law school wasn't an option for me. Pursuing an MBA with the intent of climbing the corporate ladder was uninspiring. Working the seventy to ninety hours a week it would take to become a super sales person just might kill me. My family wasn't rich, so inheritance was out of the question. And the thought of purchasing the winning lottery ticket? As exhilarating as it sounds, let's just say the odds were not good enough on which to gamble my future.

Fortunately, the most appealing path to wealth was also the path where the odds of joining the wealthy one percent were the best. Perhaps that's why more of the wealthy one percent choose this path? Success leaves clues! So, I decided I would start a business and take the profits and invest them in real estate. In addition to embarking on this path myself, I launched a website (www.EntrepreneurGrads.com) for the sole purpose of saving new high school and college grads the twenty adult years it took me to figure out this simple formula. The website provides access to a "plug-n-play" system for those just getting started in life. One of my dreams is for every American to be exposed to this information so that they can literally pick their retirement age. It could be 65, 45, or yes, even 25. This is only one way I am paying my knowledge and experience forward.

It was an easy decision to embark on this new path of business ownership and real estate investing, but the analytical side of me wanted to understand what it was that business ownership and real estate investing had in common. Why are they the most sure-fire path to our nation's wealthy one percent? I discovered two commonalities: thoughts and leverage.

Think Rich

All of a sudden, it was no wonder the biggest selling book on personal development is Napoleon Hill's *Think and Grow Rich*. It's no wonder the biggest selling audio recording in the personal development industry is Earl Nightingale's *The Strangest Secret* (the secret being *You are what you think about)*. The rich definitely think differently, and I'm not referring exclusively to "positive thinking." They simply know things that everyone else does not. If you aren't doing what they're doing, you don't know. The rich were taught and raised differently. Rich parents teach their kids to be rich. Poor parents teach their kids to be poor. Not intentionally, of course; and there are exceptions to the rule, but simply put, people teach what they know.

Here's an idea of how the thought process is different between the rich and the poor. A poor person might say, "I can't afford it," while the rich person might say, "How can I afford it?" It's a subtle difference, but remember the power of questions? A question searches for an answer, and the brain will answer any question asked of it. A statement is final. Another example is that a poor person might ask, "How much will this cost me?" while the rich person would ask a more empowering question, "How much will this make me?" Be careful what you ask the brain, for it will provide an answer—every time.

I've noticed that poor people will make up their minds slowly and change them quickly. The poor person frequently will respond to a sound investment opportunity, "Let me think about it." Rich people will make up their minds quickly and change them slowly. In response to the same investment scenario, you will more often hear the rich person say, "I'll take it, unless I change my mind." The thoughts of the rich and the poor are distinctly different.

Here's a real life example. Imagine a poor person and a rich person both earned an extra $30,000 to purchase a new car. The poor person has been taught their entire life that debt is bad, so they stroll down to the dealership and lay down all $30,000 for the new car. They own the car free and clear, no monthly payments. But, what happens the instant they drive off the lot? The car can lose up to thirty percent of its value the second it hits the street. The $30,000 investment is now worth $20,000 and depreciating by the day.

The rich person has different thoughts. Their first phone call isn't to the car dealer, it's likely to somebody like their real estate agent or their CPA or financial mentor. The rich person would probably lay down the $30,000 on a cash-producing asset, like a rental property. They would then proceed down to the car dealer and possibly lease the car. Now being a landlord, the rich person can 1) Use the cash flow from the rental property to pay for the car lease, 2) get a significant tax deduction on the car lease as a business owner (landlord=business owner), and 3) experience the appreciation and significant tax deductions that accompany the rental real estate. The rich person is essentially getting paid to drive their new car through tax breaks and holding an appreciating asset. To me, that adequately demonstrates the differences in thinking. The poor person and rich person both had the same $30,000 to spend, yet their thoughts and actions were entirely different. As a result, the poor stay poor and the rich get richer.

Leverage

The second commonality the rich share is their knowledge, and use of, leverage. It's the primary reason the rich can earn ten times, one hundred times, a thousand times what the poor can, even though they both have the same twenty-four hours in a day. As we go through life, we're all constantly leveraging or being leveraged. It's always one or the other. The rich are rich because they have learned to tip the scale in their favor when it comes to leveraging. They will leverage other people's efforts, money, experience, education, intelligence, and ideas. There are countless examples, but a basic one is when you go to work every day. Is your boss making money off of your efforts? If so, you are being leveraged. If you are making money off of his efforts, you are the boss.

You don't have to be the boss to experience the benefits of leverage. Ask yourself this: "When I go to work for money, does it return the favor?" What do you spend more of your money on, assets or liabilities? In their simplest forms, an *asset* is something that puts money in your pocket, and a *liability* is something that takes money out of your pocket. Poor people spend their money on liabilities. Rich people spend their money on assets and then let their assets pay for their liabilities. The $30,000 car example earlier demonstrates this perfectly. The rental property (asset) was leveraged to pay for the car (liability).

When it comes to investing money, the leverage concept really begins to pick up steam. Just as America's poor and middle class were taught to go to school, get good grades and get a good job, they were taught to invest their money in "safe, low-risk" investments like stocks, bonds and mutual funds. If you were to take $10,000 and invest it in a mutual fund that averaged a 6.34% annual return, at the end of thirty years it will have compounded to $66,658.21. By the way, a financial planner who could produce that type of return over thirty years would be a superstar in his industry and assuredly end up a rich man himself.

Let's take that same $10,000 and invest it using some moderate "real world" leverage. Leveraging it into a $200,000 piece of rental real estate, over the same thirty years and the same rate of return of 6.34%, that $10,000 investment would have grown to $1,333,164.27. $66,658.21 invested in stocks, bonds and mutual funds vs. $1,333,164.27 leveraged in real estate? That's the power of leverage. Again, it's no wonder the gap between the rich and the poor gets wider and wider. The poor's money, invested in stocks, bonds and mutual funds, will double every seven to eight years. The rich will double their money using leverage every seven to eight *months*. Leverage is a powerful thing! Further, what this example doesn't show is that this was a rental property, meaning the tenant paid off the mortgage. It doesn't show the positive cash flow the property produced, and it doesn't show the tax benefits either (and they're substantial). Real estate rocks, by the way (just in case it isn't evident in this example).

Work Your Passion

Being a business owner and real estate investor allows you to take your thoughts, turn them into a business, and reap the far-reaching financial benefits of leverage. What's the best business to start, you may be thinking? The best business to start is the one that excites you, because it is the one you'll do. When I'm asked this question, I immediately ask, "What do you like to do? Do you have any hobbies?" Work is what you're doing when you wished you were doing something else, so my recommendation is to **pick your passion**. If you can turn it into a business, you'll never work again. Visit http://VisionToVenture.com for a complete step-by-step system on how to turn your passion into a profitable business, systemize it, and ultimately sell it (if you want to, of course).

Another business start-up option might be to choose an existing business system in the form of a **franchise**. By Googling "franchise," you should be able to identify a legitimate franchise within the scope of your passion or interests. Going into business via a franchise was something I once considered, but I found most reputable franchises to be accompanied by heavy start-up costs and several years to break even. Not all, but most. Finding the right match between my interests and initial investment didn't pan out.

A third option would be to explore the world of **direct sales or network marketing**. Network marketing is quickly becoming a staple in the business world as more and more respectable businesses of services and products adopt this businesses model. In fact, if Donald Trump lost his fortune tomorrow, he is on record as saying he would climb his way back to the top through network marketing. He recommends budding entrepreneurs give it a go as well. Not only is it a sound business model, it is an excellent environment to test yourself, to see if being a business owner is the right thing for you. Within network marketing, a system is already in place so you can hit the ground running. The inconveniences that accompany a franchise of manning a storefront, managing employees, and keeping track of inventory are typically absent.

There are countless companies to choose from. So, how do you choose? Based off my experience, I would recommend the following before making a final decision:

1. Pick a product that interests you, and more importantly one you would purchase and use yourself. If you don't believe in the product, your customers won't either; and you won't last.

2. Meet as many people within the company as you can. Keep your antennae up for "shadiness," over-embellishments, half-truths, and specifically, flat-out lies. Trust your gut on this one, trust your first instincts and trust them fast. A good indicator is to listen to the individuals pitching the product. If you hear something along the lines of "Our product will make a blind man see," "Our product will make you rich overnight," or "There's no work involved, it's easy," head for the door.

3. If the compensation plan requires you to recruit a small country, run. It will be great practice to attempt such a feat,

but the effort is futile. The promise of the "residual dream" is a "residual lie" if you didn't get in on the bottom floor with this type of compensation plan. The sales process in every company is the same. You will be required to do the exact same activities (See the people, Tell the story, Build for events, Follow-up) to produce your success, so pick the compensation plan that pays the most, and the fastest.

4. Ideally, you will want to pick a company where your success within the company is not dependent on your ability to sell the product. Your chances of success are far greater within a dual-income opportunity, meaning you can generate income selling the product, but you can also do so by using the product. There aren't many companies that satisfy all of these criteria.

Doing-over in network marketing can be frustrating and exhausting, so take your time to make the right choice. I was able to find a great company that did meet all of these criteria. If you can't find one that suits you, you're free to take a look at the one I chose and work with me.

www.EpicProfessionals.com/income

After you're up and running and producing massive amounts of income in your chosen business, the second step of getting to the wealthy one percent is to invest your profits in real estate. By the way, if you're unable to identify a business that excites you, real estate investing can be your business as well as your investing strategy. The reason is that real estate produces two types of income, *active* and *passive*. As your business, you can produce active income through real estate investing strategies like rehabbing, fix n' flipping, wholesaling and optioning. It makes for a great business. It made enough sense to me that it is a second business of mine (www.AlbinoDino.com).

Simultaneously, you will always want to keep an eye on the long-term strategy of buy n' hold. The buy n' hold strategy is ultimately what will produce your wealth. Your wealth will be produced through appreciation, tax benefits, and passive income (i.e. positive cash flow).

Over time, real estate has always proven to appreciate (6.34% over the last forty years, since 1968). The future will be no different, and you don't have to take only my word for it. The concept of supply and demand rules the world's economy, and real estate is no exception. The supply (land) is fixed; we're not making any more. The demand (people), however, is another story. We continue to make people – a lot of people. Did you know that in 2007 more than twice the number of babies were born than in 1956, the peak year of the baby-boomers? The demand continues to increase year by year. When demand goes up, so does value.

Did I mention earlier that real estate *rocks*?

The demand for real estate is already in place. We simply have to wait for each generation – each generation being larger than the previous – to come of home-buying age. I suppose this is what Mark Twain meant when he said, "Don't wait to buy real estate; buy real estate and wait." Appreciation is a certainty, but it's certain it will have its ups and downs along the way, also. "How do you time the market?" I'm frequently asked. My answer is simple: "You don't." One would need a crystal ball to do so. I don't have one. Please call me if you do.

The hedge against the ups and downs in the market is something called cash flow. Cash flow is the difference between a property's income and a property's expenses. I don't think it has to be said that you want this number to be positive, but I will just in case. You want a property to always produce more income than it costs you to hold on to. This way you can heed Twain's advice and wait for appreciation in comfort and without financial stress.

As long as a property is paying you to hold on to it, you can't lose. To join the wealthy one percent, you will want to constantly monitor, and grow, your positive cash flow. The reason being is once that number exceeds your monthly expenses, you have options. You can retire or continue to work, but you have the luxury to work every day because you *want* to, not because you *have* to. I have found that getting up and going to work because I want to produces a far different, and greater, result than going to work because I have to.

Through real estate you have access to appreciation, passive income, the power of leverage, and America's ultimate tax incentive. Did you know most Americans can virtually eliminate their tax liability with the purchase of just a couple of investment properties? Whatever your tax liability, consult your CPA, and you'll likely find that rental real estate will reduce your annual tax bill significantly, if not all together (yes, it's possible).

Did I say earlier that real estate *rocks*?

Passive Income

Rental real estate is a great source of passive income. But there are others. Royalties from books, music, and software also produce passive income. Storage facilities, vending machines, franchising, the licensing of your ideas, and the right network marketing companies can produce great passive income as well. Whatever you choose for your passive income stream (and I encourage you to pick more than one), you will want to know that financial freedom is almost impossible without it. Passive income is a must, and it must be a focus if you ever expect to be financially free. To help you explore the abundant possibilities there are in creating passive positive cash flow, I have set up a free resource website for you: http://CashflowSavvy.com.

There are a million different ways to make a million bucks and if you look for it, you will find your way. In concluding this chapter, I want you to walk away with these thoughts:

1. Money is not evil. It is okay to want it and earn it.
2. Business ownership and real estate investing offer the greatest possibilities for you to get rich. For alternative paths, see Ken Fisher's book *The Ten Roads to Riches*, but after reading it, I believe you will agree with me.
3. You will never be financially free without positive passive income.

To your Do Over success...

Matt

CPSIA information can be obtained
at www.ICGtesting.com
Printed in the USA
BVOW09s0747310517

485610BV00001B/25/P